"Any young person will find inspiration in her story to overcome whatever barrier comes their way and to realize their dreams just as she has. I only wished I had the chance to read her story when I was reaching for my dreams!"

—MARLEE MATLIN,
Academy Award–winning
actress and activist

"For the first time, I see myself in someone else. Judy's lifelong fight and fierce advocacy around disability justice have undeniably paved the way for me to achieve what I have today. . . . A must-read for all young people."

—ALI STROKER,
Tony Award–winning actress

"Fun, exciting, and honest. This isn't just a story that disabled children will love; it's a story about what is possible when we fight for ourselves and each other. It is a story about how tenacity, strength, the power of community, and the willingness to fight for what matters can start a revolution."

—KEAH BROWN,
author of *The Pretty One*

"Judy's advocacy for disability rights began as a fight for her own future and then, as a leader of the movement, spanned the nation and the globe."

—HILLARY CLINTON

"I met Judy Heumann almost four decades ago, and her writing, activist skills, and kindness helped me to see this simple truth. Her life story as an activist will enlighten readers everywhere."

—GLORIA STEINEM

"A marvelous memoir by a disability hero who has paved the way for so many of us. This book will inspire a new generation of disability rights activists and guide future leaders as we work toward a barrier-free world."

—HABEN GIRMA,
author of the bestseller
*Haben: The Deafblind Woman
Who Conquered Harvard Law*

"A powerful yet tender memoir from one of the most important figures in disability rights history. Judy's story made me laugh, cringe, and perhaps most importantly, it lit a fire in me to fight harder for disability rights."

—SHANE BURCAW,
author of *Laughing at My Nightmare*

"For everyone who cares about human rights around the world, Judith Heumann's moving story and message of belonging is also a powerful call to action."

—YETNEBERSH NIGUSSIE,
disability rights activist

ROLLING
WARRIOR

WARRIOR

THE INCREDIBLE,
SOMETIMES AWKWARD,
TRUE STORY OF A
REBEL GIRL ON WHEELS
WHO HELPED
SPARK
A REVOLUTION

· · · · · · ·

JUDITH HEUMANN
WITH KRISTEN JOINER

BEACON PRESS
BOSTON

Beacon Press
Boston, Massachusetts
www.beacon.org

Beacon Press books
are published under the auspices of
the Unitarian Universalist Association of Congregations.

24 23 22 21   8 7 6 5 4 3 2 1

This book is printed on acid-free paper that meets the uncoated paper
ANSI/NISO specifications for permanence as revised in 1992.

Text design and composition by Kim Arney

Library of Congress Cataloging-in-Publication Data
Names: Heumann, Judith E., author. | Joiner, Kristen, author.
Title: Rolling warrior : the incredible, sometimes awkward, true story of a
    rebel girl on wheels who helped spark a revolution / Judith Heumann
    with Kristen Joiner.
Description: Boston : Beacon Press, 2021. | Audience: Ages 10 and up |
    Audience: Grades 4-6
Identifiers: LCCN 2021003306 (print) | LCCN 2021003307 (ebook) |
    ISBN 9780807003596 (trade paperback) | ISBN 9780807003602 (ebook)
Subjects: LCSH: Heumann, Judith E.—Juvenile literature. | Human rights
    workers—United States—Biography—Juvenile literature. | People with
    disabilities—United States—Biography—Juvenile literature.
Classification: LCC JC571 .H493 2021 (print) | LCC JC571 (ebook) |
    DDC 362.4092 [B]—dc23
LC record available at https://lccn.loc.gov/2021003306
LC ebook record available at https://lccn.loc.gov/2021003307

*To Marca Bristo, a dear friend,
and to the other relentless disabled warriors who
have passed on. Their legacies are living on as new
leaders take their rightful place in our movement
and continue to fight for equality.*

—JUDITH HEUMANN

■　■　■

*To Julian, Oliver, and Olivia.
You amaze me every day.*

—KRISTEN JOINER

CIVIL RIGHTS, *plural noun*

1. the rights of citizens to political and social freedom and equality.

—*Oxford English Dictionary*

CONTENTS

Prologue xi

PART ONE 1

CHAPTER ONE Yelling at blank walls 3

CHAPTER TWO Time for rest hour, kids 17

CHAPTER THREE Sorry, if you could just hide behind everyone else that would be great 25

CHAPTER FOUR If you're not busy, can you help me into bed? 35

CHAPTER FIVE You want me to what? 45

CHAPTER SIX The last drop 53

CHAPTER SEVEN Are you Judy Heumann? 55

CHAPTER EIGHT The fight 63

CHAPTER NINE Am I reading correctly? 69

PART TWO **THREE YEARS LATER** 79

CHAPTER TEN Weird sleepover 81

CHAPTER ELEVEN And suddenly, we're visible 95

CHAPTER TWELVE Dinner tonight courtesy of the Black Panthers 105

CHAPTER THIRTEEN   The government threatens
                       us with bombs   113

CHAPTER FOURTEEN   We threaten the government with
                      more sleepovers   121

CHAPTER FIFTEEN   House party at Califano's   129

CHAPTER SIXTEEN   There are no accessible bathrooms
                      in the White House   139

CHAPTER SEVENTEEN   Please don't ignore us or we will come
                      to your Sunday school   145

CHAPTER EIGHTEEN   Power to the people   153

PART THREE   FOUR YEARS LATER   157

CHAPTER NINETEEN   Thirty-six million of us   159

EPILOGUE   And next   175

                      Acknowledgments   187
                      Credits   191

The thing to know about me is this: if I'd been born just ten years earlier and my parents hadn't left Germany when they did, I would have been killed by Nazis. Hitler considered us "life unworthy of life."

If you were a young disabled child in Nazi Germany in the 1930s, the doctors recommended that your parents hand you over to a special children's clinic where you were either starved or poisoned. When the Nazis expanded the program to include older disabled children, the doctors experimented with gassing them. Five thousand disabled kids were used as a means to test new innovative ways of killing masses of people. Which meant that we were the experiment for a campaign that was responsible for the systematic dehumanization and murder of almost twenty million people.

My Jewish grandparents sent my father away from Germany before World War II, when he was fourteen, to go live with his uncle and two brothers in Brooklyn. He never saw his parents again. But, in some way, he was the lucky one. My mother was only twelve when she was sent away to live with people she'd never met before. She never saw her parents again either. I guess that my grandparents on both sides were worried enough about Hitler to send their kids away but didn't think it was going to get as bad as it did. A lot of people didn't know how bad it was going to get.

So you can see why, when I got sick at one year old and it became clear that I was never going to walk again and the doctor told my parents to put me in an institution, my parents were like, "No way."

Institutionalization was the status quo for people with disabilities when I was a child in 1949. You basically got put in a building, looked after by nurses, and your parents weren't even encouraged to visit you. There were all kinds of bad things happening in the institutions to people with disabilities, which nobody was talking about. It wasn't until I was in my twenties, in the 1960s, that it came out that disabled people were getting locked up, beaten, starved, and used like guinea pigs for medical experiments. We were considered mentally and physically defective. Disabled kids brought stigma to the family. People thought when someone in your family had a disability it was because someone had done something wrong.

Years later, when people would say that what we did changed the world, I said this: "All we did was refuse to believe that we were the problem."

In order to understand what really happened, though, let me tell you a story about what the world was like then—before we mobilized our army, took over the San Francisco Federal Building, and faced down the US government.

So I'll begin at the beginning.

ROLLING
WARRIOR

PART ONE

CHAPTER ONE

YELLING AT BLANK WALLS

I got sick when I was just eighteen months old.

Polio is a virus, kind of like the flu. Most people who get it are fine after a week or two, but some end up paralyzed and not able to move. I was one of the paralyzed people. When I got better and the polio was out of my system, I still couldn't move my legs or lift my arms.

Well, actually, that's not entirely true. I can lift my arms a little, just not very far. I can lift a glass and drink out of it. I can hold a fork and feed myself. I can dial numbers on my phone, type on my computer, and move my baby toe. All the important things.

Here is what I can't do: I can't go to the bathroom by myself. I can't dress myself, and I can't walk. I use a wheelchair to get around.

I was born just after World War II ended. Back then, there were several polio epidemics. Everyone was scared of catching it. People didn't know how it was

Me when I was little

spread, and there was no vaccine yet, so lots of kids got sick. Nowadays, most people get a shot for it, which is why hardly anyone gets it anymore.

For me, polio was no big deal. I was so little I don't remember feeling sick and I don't remember ever not using a wheelchair.

But apparently for everyone else, me getting paralyzed was a big deal. I can understand how this would have been pretty big for my parents since I almost died and then they had to adjust the house to make it work for a kid who couldn't walk. But once they made some adjustments, it was just normal life again. What I don't really get is how perfect strangers would assume that me becoming paralyzed was a tragedy.

One day, I was considered a "normal" kid, because I could walk and the next, I was considered a "disabled" kid because I couldn't. People still talk about that day as if I became an entirely different person, even though I was still the same kid.

By the time I was six, I was rolling around on my own. This was an extremely strenuous task. Not because I couldn't walk and my arms weren't fully functional—although I can see why you could think that—but because everything in the world had been created as if we didn't exist.

Streets had curbs (with no ramps), houses had steps, motorized wheelchairs weren't around yet – and you get the idea. So, this means that I had a manual wheelchair (which required one to have strong arms to push, which I of course didn't have), and, on a daily basis, confronted curbs and steps that were as impossible to scale as the Great Wall of China.

You know how some people think that if you pretend something doesn't exist, it will just go away?

Even though thousands of kids were getting polio and ending up paralyzed, no one was saying, "Hey, let's make little electric wheelchairs so kids can see their friends!" No one was thinking about it, and we weren't even the first disabled kids in history. Because for as long as there have been humans, there have been people being born blind or deaf or with physical disabilities that make it hard to control how you move, or with dwarfism or some kind of intellectual disability— or some other kind of thing. There have also been kids like me, who become disabled after we're born— through an illness, accident, or whatever. I think the logic here was something along the lines of: disability is a blight on society; if you ignore it, it will go away.

But I can tell you right now that disability is a normal part of life and if we wish it away that would mean: (1) we'd all have to go away because disability is part of being human; (2) most of my friends would have to go away and that would be sad because they are some of the nicest, smartest people I know; and (3) no more Harry Potter because Daniel Radcliffe has a disability. But I digress. Let's go back to the time I was little and in a manual wheelchair.

This is what it took to make a normal, everyday trip to my friend Arlene's house when I was six.

PHASE ONE:
1. Get my mom to push me down our ramp to the sidewalk.
2. Inch my way along the sidewalk. The key to getting to Arlene's was this super tiny incline. If I could get myself to the top of it, I could use the momentum to coast down the other side.
3. Land at Arlene's. (P.S. Arlene lived next door.)

Once I got to Arlene's steps, I launched Phase Two.

Now you'd think that inching my way up a tiny incline would be the awkward part of this expedition—but no. The awkward part was yet to come.

PHASE TWO:
1. Sit by myself on the sidewalk, staring at Arlene's red brick house. (If the car was in the driveway, I knew they were home.)

2. Prepare to yell.
3. Shout at the top of my lungs, "ARLENE! COME OUT AND PLAY!"

We lived on one of those streets where there were tons of kids and everyone knows each other. I was the only kid in a wheelchair, but this meant literally nothing to us. We were little and we just figured things out, like you do when you're little. If everyone was roller skating, we put roller skates over my shoes and I skated in my chair. If everyone was jumping rope, I turned the rope for the kids who were jumping. We didn't even think about it. Me being in a wheelchair just felt like me having straight hair when Mary had curly. Sometimes I think kids are so much smarter than adults.

■ ■ ■

But inching around in a world pretending that disabled kids don't exist was not the worst thing about having a disability when I was little. I'll tell you the worst thing. I was five. It was September. I had that fluttery feeling. You know, the one you get when something big's happening. It was the first day of kindergarten. I picked out what I wanted to wear the night before and got my mom to lay it out on my bed. That night I couldn't sleep.

When we got to school the next morning, my mom pulled my chair up the steps backward and pushed me into the building. I looked around at everything, trying to figure out where my class was, checking out all the other students. Everything was so alive. I barely noticed when a man stopped my mom in the hallway.

I knew something was up, though, when I saw the look on my mom's face. Her mouth got tight and her eyes turned dark. Then she turned me around, tipped my wheelchair back, and bumped me down the steps out of school. When I saw we were going back home, the butterflies in my stomach turned into rocks. But I was quiet. When my dad got home that night, my parents had a long whispery conversation, after which my dad's shoulders got really straight in that way they do when he's very angry.

I didn't go to school the next day. Or the next day. Or the next.

Then my mom told me I wasn't going to go to school. I was going to stay home with her instead. What she didn't tell me was that the principal had said I'd be a "fire hazard." Which meant that if there was a fire, he thought I'd block the teachers from getting the other kids out of the school.

I didn't understand why I had to stay home with my little brother, Joey, while everyone I knew went to school. It made no sense. I could tell my mom thought so too. But her eyes just looked sad. Like the brown leaves falling off the trees in our yard.

The next day, I sat by the window and watched Arlene and Mary and all the kids on our block walk down the street together. They were talking and laughing. I swallowed really hard and turned my head away. I still didn't really understand why I wasn't going with them, but didn't want to make my mom feel bad.

I know now that my parents didn't get why I couldn't go to school in a wheelchair—*especially* in America. My mom thought there was a solution to any problem if you just tried hard enough. She was tiny and my dad called her Mighty Mite.

One of the first things my mom did was try to get me into the Jewish day school near our house. The principal told her I could go to the school if I learned Hebrew first.

So my mom decided I was going to learn Hebrew. Somehow, she found a friend of a friend to teach me and took me for lessons, literally every single day for one summer. Until (according to my mother) I spoke Hebrew better than the other kids. Then she called the school back and told him I'd learned Hebrew. But the principal, who was probably in shock that I'd actually done it, backtracked.

"I'm terribly sorry but it's just not going to work," he told my mom.

At the beginning of what should have been my first grade, the board of education called my mother and told her they would send a teacher to my home for instruction. This was the beginning of Mrs. Campfield, who started coming to our house twice a week for about two and a half hours. During those hours, I was supposed to learn to read and do math and do all the other things my friends had already been doing for two years. Mrs. Campfield was nice, but when you compare my two and a half hours to my friends' twenty-five hours a week in school, the idea that I could catch up with them was ridiculous.

It was around then that my parents started to get really worried that the board of education had no intention of educating me. Which was actually the truth. By that time, I'm sure some of the board members were getting tired of my mom trying to figure out a solution for me. They probably thought, "Why hasn't that lady gotten the memo? Disabled kids don't *need* to go to school. They're supposed to stay home or go to an institution."

It felt really weird when my little brother Joey started school. Every morning I watched him on his way to school. When I saw him getting ready, reaching for the door, I wished I could go too.

Have you ever had the feeling that something doesn't make sense but because everyone around you is acting like it does, you just kind of accept it?

That was me.

I processed it this way: Mary and the Catholic kids on my block went to Catholic school, Arlene and the Protestant kids and my brother went to public school, and I went to "school" at home. We all went to different schools.

And that worked for me. At least, until the day of the boy.

■ ■ ■

Arlene was pushing me around the corner to the store. When we crossed the street in front of my mother's doctor's house, some kids appeared, walking toward us. Arlene shifted my wheelchair to the side when one of the kids stopped right in front of me. A boy.

"Are you sick?" he asked me.

I stared at him.

"What?" I said.

"Are you sick?" his voice boomed.

I shook my head, confused.

"Are. You. Sick?" he asked, slowing the words way down.

The words echoed in my head. All I could hear was . . . sick . . . sick . . . sick . . . sick.

This boy would not leave me alone. I wanted to hide.

"ARE YOU SICK?!" he shouted.

I remembered my mother's doctor's house was behind me. That was it! He thinks I'm going to the doctor. But then I thought, "Wait a minute. He's not *my* doctor!" And I *wasn't* sick. I knew I wasn't.

But then why was he asking me that? I became uncertain. *Was* I sick?

Slowly, I saw myself through his eyes. All around me, light shifted. Shadows, words, thoughts, half-heard conversations tumbled into my head.

Everything in my life finally clicked.

I couldn't go to this school, I couldn't go to that school. I couldn't do this, I couldn't do that, I couldn't walk up the stairs, I couldn't open doors, I couldn't even cross the street.

I *was* different. But I'd always known that. It wasn't that.

It was the world and how it saw me.

The world thought I was sick.

Sick people stayed home in bed. They didn't go to school. They weren't expected to go outside, to be a part of things, to be a part of the world.

I wasn't expected to be a part of the world.

I felt nauseated that everyone else had known this but me. Had they kept it from me?

The feeling settled in as a cold ball deep in my stomach.

Was it sunny or cloudy? I don't know. I remember Arlene was pushing me, we were going to the store to buy candy, and we were chatting.

And I was a butterfly, becoming a caterpillar.

■ ■ ■

That night, I said nothing to my family. At dinner I was quiet. I ate and went to bed. The next morning, I woke up, had breakfast, and went outside. I played jump rope with Mary and Arlene, Patsy and Beth, Teddy and all the kids on the block. We talked about all the same things. On Monday my brother went to school, Mrs. Campfield came, my brother came home, and we went to Hebrew school. It was all the same. But everything felt entirely different.

■ ■ ■

Not long after the incident with the boy, my mom finally found a school that would take me. Well technically, it wasn't a school, it was a program for disabled kids. It was called Health Conservation 21.

Why Health Conservation 21? Why *health*? Why *conservation*? Why not *Education Take-Over-the-World*?

I'll tell you why: there was no good reason. Our name was a stereotype.

We were not sick.

The name Health Conservation gave you the (erroneous) idea that we had medical problems that needed to be solved and once we were cured, we'd be able to participate in society. It was, in other words, society's way of saying, "It's not us, it's you."

Well, I knew I wasn't going to walk again and, frankly, I didn't care. I just wanted what every other kid in the world wants: to go to school, see my friends, and have fun.

■ ■ ■

The other thing I need to tell you about Health Conservation 21 was that the board of education had required that I be screened for admission to the program.

Here is a tip: all kids living in the United States have the right to a free public education.

But there I was, being assessed for my ability to go to a public education program. If I didn't pass their test, I wouldn't be allowed to go. Like nobody else I knew.

■ ■ ■

Luckily, I passed this test and started school in the middle of the fourth grade.

Even though I was nine years old and I'd been through this before, I was excited. Again, I picked out what I wanted to wear for my first day and, again, I asked my mom to lay it out on my bed.

But this day went very differently.

CHAPTER TWO

TIME FOR
REST HOUR, KIDS

There was a woman standing at the classroom door. "You must be Judy. I'm Mrs. Parker," she said. She seemed nice. She asked me to sit at a desk with a girl she introduced as Shelley, who used a wheelchair too. There were only eight or nine students in the class. I tried to look at everyone without looking like I was checking people out. Every single kid was in a wheelchair. I'd never met any other disabled kids before. It felt funny, kind of like I was looking in a weird mirror.

Wow, I thought. They must have all the same problems I do. They must get stopped by curbs too and sit outside their friends' houses and yell. I wondered if people thought they were sick.

They all seemed to be different ages, though, which confused me. This was fourth grade?

Okay, I'd never been in school before, but I knew that certain grades meant you were a certain age. My little brother, Joey, started kindergarten when he was five, first grade when he was six, and second grade when he was seven. But the tall girl in my new class looked like she had to be at least sixteen or seventeen. Uh-oh, I thought, am I going to be way behind everyone else?

■ ■ ■

I pretty quickly discovered I wasn't. The worksheets Mrs. Parker handed out repeated what I'd already done with Mrs. Campfield, and Mrs. Parker spoke really slowly.

I was reading a book while some of the other kids finished the worksheets when Mrs. Parker told us to put our books away for lunch. All the kids started pulling out their lunches. I sat at my desk and ate my lunch next to Shelley. Chicken sandwich with apple slices. Shelley was pretty quiet. We didn't say much to each other.

I had just finished my sandwich and drunk my milk when Mrs. Parker stood up.

"Okay, class, please put your lunch items away and get ready for rest time," she said.

What?? Was she joking? A *rest* hour? I was *nine*! I stopped napping when I was *four*.

I looked around quickly to see who else was laughing. All the kids had already closed their eyes, even the girls who looked like they were sixteen or seventeen.

Mrs. Parker turned out the lights.

Fine. I tried to sit quietly in my wheelchair with my eyes closed too.

Finally, after what seemed like long enough for my toenails to have grown an inch, Mrs. Parker turned the lights back on and handed out another worksheet. When we were done, Mrs. Parker snapped her book shut and told us to start packing up our things.

That was my first day of school.

■ ■ ■

The next day, I went back. And the next. And the next.

Now it was Joey *and* me getting our backpacks and rushing around every morning before school, and I *loved* it.

Some of the kids had had polio. Other kids had muscular dystrophy or cerebral palsy. The kids who had cerebral palsy couldn't always control their hands or arms, which meant they couldn't necessarily feed themselves. Lots of kids needed help eating their lunch. So I sat and helped them.

It turned out that the tall girl in the corner who looked sixteen *was* actually sixteen and didn't know how to read. Neither did the other older girl. I started helping them with their reading.

I had new friends to hang out with. I felt like cheering. Some of my new friends didn't speak very clearly, but I didn't care. Why wouldn't I take the time to listen to them? They were funny and smart, and I liked them.

But here's where you might be thinking, What about the sixteen- and seventeen-year-old-kids in your class? What's up with that?

I soon learned a lot about our situation at Health Conservation 21.

We were the "special education kids." Our school was in the basement of a school for "normal kids," who we called the "kids upstairs." We were kept completely separate from them, and our days were totally different.

The kids upstairs were in school about two hours longer than us every day. They were given tests and grades and lots of attention because the adults wanted to be sure they had learned enough to go to high school and then, ideally, college.

You might be thinking, "Lucky you!" Because lots of kids complain about having to go to school every day.

But the thing is, school is how a society makes sure that everyone knows what they need to know, to be able to get a job, or do whatever they want to do. In America, school is considered so important that it's been compulsory since 1918. "Compulsory" is just a fancy word that means everyone has to do it.

Well, I should say, everyone except us.

Nobody expected us to learn. Nobody tested us or gave us grades to make sure we were learning what we needed for high school or college. They didn't expect us to go to high school or college, or even middle school.

They expected nothing of us.

■ ■ ■

We were supposed to stay in Health Conservation 21 until we were, yes, you guessed it, twenty-one. Then we were supposed to go into these things called "sheltered workshops," which is where they made you do menial work and paid you almost nothing. This is why there were kids in my class who didn't know how to read. Apparently, you don't need to know how to read to do menial jobs in a sheltered workshop.

We were smart. We noticed the difference between how people treated us and how people treated the kids upstairs. We talked about it a lot. We spent hours trying to figure out *why*. Why did people see us so differently from the kids upstairs? We didn't *feel* different, at least not on the inside. We only felt like we were being *treated* differently, which made us feel strange, almost like we deserved it.

At school, Frieda and Linda were my best friends. They were both Jewish, like me, but they hadn't had polio. They had something called muscular dystrophy, which made their muscles too weak to get around without a wheelchair. Frieda's parents were refugees too. They'd survived World War II by hiding in sewers in Poland.

We discovered that all three of us hated the same things—like that fact that we couldn't reach the clothes in our closets. I'd always felt like I was the only ten-year-old in the world who still had her mom picking out her clothes. Like that horrible itchy green dress she seemed to like so much.

It also drove us crazy when people stared at us. When Frieda and I inched along the sidewalk in our wheelchairs, we talked back to the starers.

"Take a picture—it will last longer!" we said and killed ourselves laughing.

■ ■ ■

The year after I started school, I also started summer camp. Camp was just like school, meaning it was only for disabled kids. We had these awesome teenage counselors who played the guitar and organized massive games of baseball. We had big dance parties and didn't have to worry about people staring at our dancing. But this wasn't the best thing about camp. I'll tell you what the most amazing thing about camp was.

Have you ever thought what it would feel like if you had to ask someone for help every time you

wanted a glass of water? Or dropped a pencil? Or had
to go to the bathroom really bad? Let me give you a
hint. You'd feel annoying, like you were always asking
for favors. Pretty soon, you'd be secretly ranking what
you needed in order of importance so you wouldn't
have to ask for too much at once.

This was my whole life, except for when I was
at camp.

At camp, the counselors were paid to do these
things for us—which, I can tell you, makes a massive
difference. Because the reality is, asking someone to do
something for you when they're not getting paid, or
when they're not required to do it, gets old, no matter
how nice that person is.

I don't know what I would have done if I hadn't
started school and camp at that time.

We were segregated and excluded, and only our
parents expected anything of us, but we had each other.

CHAPTER THREE

SORRY, IF YOU COULD JUST HIDE BEHIND EVERYONE ELSE THAT WOULD BE GREAT

I was sweaty. My pencil kept slipping out of my hand. "Everyone has to get used to taking exams sometime," I told myself, my heart pounding.

"Ha. Just not at fourteen," a voice deep inside me answered. Great, I thought. No help there. Thank you very much, inner voice.

I was officially a high school student at Sheepshead Bay in Brooklyn. My mom and a gang of other disabled kids' moms had successfully pushed the New York City Board of Education into allowing some of us to go to high school. I was the first student from Health Conservation 21 to go. And since I'd never been given any tests, grades, or anything like that, this meant that for the first time in my life, I was dealing with real exams and real grades. Which at fourteen, I can officially say, is terrifying.

I took a deep breath. The minute hand on the clock ticked so loudly that I jumped. I looked up at it. Thirty minutes left and I had to pee. Awesome. I knew I shouldn't have had that glass of water at lunch. I'd skipped drinking at breakfast so I thought it would be okay. Obviously, I was wrong.

I put my head back down and kept writing.

The bell rang just as I was finishing my last sentence. Around me, the room erupted with twenty-five kids slamming books.

"Hey, Scott, how about that exam, huh?"

"Kim, wait for me!"

"John, you going to football after school?"

I tried to look like I had something really important to do with my pencil. I didn't know any of them. I was getting bused an hour and a half across Brooklyn to Sheepshead Bay because my neighborhood high school wasn't accessible. Sheepshead Bay was basically a fishing village on the edge of New York City. You can imagine how tight the kids were. They'd all grown up swimming in the harbor together and playing baseball.

Every time the bell rang, I had to ask one of them to push me to my next class because I still only had a manual wheelchair.

I didn't want to shout for a favor over the noise, so I waited for people to leave, while I pretended to look for something in my bag. When the room felt empty, I glanced around to see who was left. Across from me, gathering her books, was a girl from my seventh-period math class. She always asked good questions. What was her name again? I tried desperately to remember. Sarah? Stella? Sally?

"Um, excuse me. Sorry. I wonder if . . . would you mind? Could I ask if you might help me get to my next class?" Oh, geez. I stumbled over my words.

"Sure!" The girl looked up at me and quickly smiled brightly. "I'm going to English. Room 312. Where are you going?"

"Oh, darnit! I'm going to room 207. History. A whole floor below. Out of your way, I'm sure. I'm sorry. I hope I don't make you late, but do you mind if we stop at the bathroom on the way? I felt a flush rise from my chest and slowly move across my face. Great. The humiliation of having to ask one of your peers to take you to class and the bathroom at fourteen years old.

"Of course!" the girl chirped, as she walked behind my wheelchair to roll me out the door.

Entering the hallway, I looked straight ahead and asked the girl her name. It was Sally. This was one of my tricks. If I focused on the girl and didn't look around, I wouldn't see the kids staring at me, wondering if they thought I was sick.

I just didn't understand how I'd come to feel so different from nondisabled kids.

My classmates at Sheepshead Bay made me uncomfortable. They moved so quickly, rushing around and making after-school plans. But not me. I got pushed to class, bused an hour and a half to and from school, and didn't even know how to start a conversation with anyone.

First of all, I was butt height. Which, as you might imagine, made talking a little awkward if someone didn't think to bend down. Second, for the first time in my life, I was in a competitive school. But on top of everything else, it seemed like nondisabled kids had a way of talking and telling jokes that I didn't get.

It was like I spoke a different language. I loved my friends from Health Conservation 21 and summer camp, but the separation between my "disabled" world and my new "regular" world made me feel like I was two different people. In my disabled world, I felt good, like I belonged. But in the regular world, I felt like an alien. The kids at Sheepshead Bay seemed like they felt awkward too, like they weren't used to talking to a kid in a wheelchair. No matter what I did, I felt like I couldn't get them to see me as a normal teenage girl.

■ ■ ■

I wasn't expected to date. No one, not even my parents, expected anyone to like me. I was "crippled." The message I got was this: no boy will ever give you a second look.

I knew what it felt like to be treated like a regular kid. At camp, I wasn't seen as sick. We had parties, played loud music, and sneaked off into the dark. So, yeah, I knew what it felt like to be treated like a normal person, and that wasn't happening at Sheepshead Bay. Which felt bad.

There were only about twenty other disabled kids at school, but we stuck together. We had time during that hour-and-a-half bus ride and a few smaller "special-ed" classes to hang out. I felt closer to them than I did to any of the nondisabled kids. They made me feel strong. The regular kids made me feel like the raisin in a bowl of candy.

One day, my high school counselor told me that I'd never get married. She was actually trying to be helpful. She told me, "You should go to college because you won't be able to count on your MRS degree." That meant, becoming a "missus," a wife.

You have to realize that this was a time when women were told to plan their lives around getting married to the best husband they could find—meaning the richest or the most handsome, or preferably both. So this woman was trying to be kind and warn me not to expect to find a husband who would take care of me, so I'd better figure out a way to support myself— and I wasn't going to be able to support myself on a high school degree, so I'd better go to college.

Funny enough, this ended up working in my favor, because I worked my butt off. So thank you, nice ableist woman, for not seeing me as a person. Although, to be fair to the Mighty Mite and my dad, they also really wanted me to go to college and not just because I had a disability.

So at high school I didn't date. I talked on the phone and I studied.

In the end, by the time I graduated, I found I'd worked so hard that I'd won an award.

I sat in the back of our van, my father driving our family to watch me get up on stage to receive my award. I couldn't stop beaming. I'd hung in there, despite the zillion favors I'd had to ask for. Glancing back from the front seat, my mom smiled at me. I knew she and my dad were proud. I mean, how many times had she been told I wasn't allowed to attend this school or that school? I'd been a "fire hazard." And yet, here I was, after all that, graduating from high school.

Pulling into a parking spot as close to the building as he could find, my dad stopped the van. Joey pushed the side door open and my brothers climbed out, while I sat and waited for my dad to lever my chair to the ground. I felt good in my purple dress and black graduate robes. My hair was all the way past my shoulders.

Inside, the giant hall was bursting with people all over the place. There were graduates in their hats and robes, getting their pictures taken, grandparents standing together, and little kids chasing each other around. My dad pushed me through the crowd toward the stage. The kids getting awards were supposed to sit on the stage so they could easily be called forward and congratulated in front of the audience.

"Sorry . . . excuse me . . . sorry . . . excuse me," my father said, and we slowly weaved our way through the hall. My mother, brothers, aunt, uncle, and cousins peeled off to find seats. From my chair I looked for the stage. But when I spotted the stairs, my heart jumped.

"Dad, there's no ramp," I said.

"Hmmmm. Maybe there's one around the back." My father pushed me to the bottom of the stairs and found a security guard.

"Excuse me, sir. Is there a ramp to access the stage? My daughter is receiving an award and she's supposed to sit on the stage." Waiting for the man to answer, my heart pounded. Please, please, please let there be a ramp. I did *not* want to get carried onto the stage in front of this massive crowd. Nor did I want to watch my father bump and lug my wheelchair up the stairs after me.

The guard looked down at me and shook his head. "No, sir, sorry. No ramp. Just stairs."

My father sighed a very quiet sigh.

He pulled my wheelchair to the side of the stairs.

"Okay, honey. I'll bring you up." He turned my chair around and started pulling me up the stairs backward. Trying to pretend I was as small as possible, not wanting to see how many people might be witnessing my awkward entry onto the stage, I squeezed my eyes shut.

Which is why I didn't notice the principal until he called out.

"Sir! Mr. Heumann! Wait a minute. Just leave Judy down here in the front row. She doesn't need to be on stage."

"What?" my father paused, halfway up the stairs. "It's no problem. I'm happy to bring her up."

"No, no, it's not necessary." The principal shook his head.

My father looked confused. My face grew hot.

"Look," my father said to the principal, "it's very easy. I'll just roll her onto the stage. It will take two minutes."

The principal looked at my father. "No," he said firmly. "Judy does not need to be on the stage. Put her in the front row." It was clear. The principal did not want me on the stage.

"Dad, let's go home," I said, my voice trembling. "I don't want to stay."

My father squared his shoulders and looked ten inches taller. He looked like the ex-Marine he was. The one who'd fought in World War II and won a Purple Heart.

He looked down at the principal, "I am going to finish pulling Judy up the stairs," enunciating every word slowly with a deathly calm. "Then I'm going to wheel her into her place, so she can receive her award on the stage. With all the other kids." I froze and looked at the principal.

For a long moment, the principal didn't speak. Finally, he conceded. "Take her up," he said turning away.

My eyes burned. "Dad," I said, "I want to go home. Take me home."

"No, Judy." My father was stern. "You are not going home. You are going to stay here. You are going to sit on the stage and receive your award. You worked hard. It is your award and you deserve it." He climbed the rest of the steps and rolled me into a spot.

I took a deep breath. He was right. This was my award and, even though not one part of me felt like it, I knew I belonged here. I straightened my headband and wiped my eyes.

As my father settled my wheelchair, the principal walked over to us.

"Put her here," he said, motioning to a place behind the rest of the students.

He did not want me to be seen.

My father clenched his jaw. But he wheeled me to the back of the stage.

"Good luck, honey. We'll be watching." Kissing the top of my head, he left. I looked out at the masses in the audience and fought back a fresh set of tears.

"I belong here," I repeated to myself silently.

When the principal called my name and started to walk to the back of the stage, I was already slowly pushing my wheelchair toward the front. I'd only made it a little way though, before he intercepted me and handed me my award.

I looked him directly in the eyes.

"Thank you," I said.

But of course, no one heard me.

CHAPTER FOUR

IF YOU'RE NOT BUSY, CAN YOU HELP ME INTO BED?

The following September, I rolled onto campus to start college at Long Island University. I wanted to be the first teacher in a wheelchair in New York City. Well, to be honest, I just wanted to be a teacher, but since there were no teachers in wheelchairs in New York City that meant I wanted to be the first one. But I couldn't tell anyone.

"Don't tell Rehab you want to be a teacher," my friends told me. "They'll tell you that you can't." Rehab, otherwise known as the US Department of Rehabilitation, helped disabled people go to college and get jobs by paying some of their expenses. They felt like this gave them the right to tell us what to do. They had a very specific idea about what we should and should not do, which was basically determined by what other people were doing. If you couldn't show

Rehab that there was someone with a disability similar to yours, doing something like what you wanted to do, then they wouldn't pay for it. Obviously, since there were no disabled teachers in New York City, there was no way they were going to let me be a teacher. So I had to major in speech therapy and minor in education on the side.

I lived in the dorms, which were little apartments where students lived at the university. My school was small, only three or four main buildings. Most of the students lived at home and took the train or bus to school every day, but I thought I'd get more out of my college experience if I lived on campus. Not to mention the fact that it would have been very difficult for me to get back and forth from home because there were no accessible buses or trains. Besides, I'd already spent what felt like half my life taking ridiculously long bus rides to school, and I was tired of it.

I was really excited to start college and live away from home for the first time. I had just one problem.

Well, to be specific, I had three problems, and they were the two steps into my dorm and the one step into the bathroom on my floor. And those three steps meant that every single time I had to go to the bathroom or wanted to go back to my room, I had to knock on someone's door, or somehow scrape around and find someone to help me.

Yes, this was incredibly awkward.

I mean, how many times do you go to the bathroom every day? Have you ever counted? I have. For you, it's probably, um . . . I'd guess ten, maybe. For me, it's usually four. On a good day, if I plan my drinking right, I can get down to three.

I immediately set out to make friends on my floor.

Here's a good thing to know: if you need help getting to the bathroom, it's a thousand times easier to ask a friend than it is to ask a stranger. I figured out who the best people to ask were pretty fast. I developed a superpower for reading people. I could tell right away who the "sure, no problem!" people were, who would almost never say no. They were the opposite of the "no way" people, who I would never in a million years ask. The hardest group was the "maybe" people. I'd only ask one of them if I was totally desperate because you just had no idea which way it was going to go with the "maybe" people—they could say yes, but they could just as easily say no.

If you think it's embarrassing to have to ask someone to help you get to the bathroom, I can tell you that having them say no takes it to a whole new level.

Luckily, I'm naturally pretty outgoing and like meeting people. It didn't take me long to get to know everyone on my floor. Everyone was really nice and went out of their way to talk to me.

But it was awkward to ask people for favors so often. It made me feel annoying, which was a bad feeling.

And then there was the bedtime issue.

Okay, I know I said I only had three problems, but that may have been a slight exaggeration for the sake of story. I mean, the truth is, I had so many issues to solve it's hard to count. In fact, my whole life every day was solving one problem after another.

I wore braces on my legs that I couldn't get off by myself, so at night I needed help with my braces, my pajamas, and getting into bed. Then, in the morning, it was the reverse. And I really didn't want my mom to live with me at college.

Before I started school, I'd asked around among my disabled friends from camp about how they'd dealt with this challenge. The solution seemed to be to find a roommate who I could pay a little to help me. I had a friend who was a year ahead of me at Long Island University and she connected me with a girl who she thought might be willing to help. Which is how I met Toni.

Toni was tall and smart. She was from New Mexico and had moved to New York for college. She agreed to be my roommate and solved my primary bedtime/ morning issue, but I still had to do complicated logistical planning every day because Toni didn't go to Long Island University—she actually went to a completely different school about an hour away. She was away all day, every day, and sometimes she had things to do and got home late at night. On those nights, I had to try to schedule someone from my floor to help me.

Did I mention I was also still inching my way around in my manual wheelchair?

Yup, I did have to ask my classmates to push me to class and anywhere else I wanted to go.

Basically, I was constantly scheduling things, like my trips to the bathroom and my bedtime, and trying to match up these different pieces of my life with people I could ask for help.

You could say that my life was a Rubik's Cube of favors.

■ ■ ■

One Saturday night I was studying in my room when someone knocked on the door. It was a girl I knew from another floor.

"Hi!" she said. "Sorry to bother you, but I was just wondering, um, we're going on a triple date and one of the women who was supposed to come can't come. Do you know anyone who is around tonight and could take her place?"

My heart skipped a beat. Was she asking me to go?

All I could think was: *Yes, yes, I am free! I would love to go!*

But then I looked at her face. My heart sank.

She didn't mean me. She meant anyone but me.

"No, not really," I said.

"Oh, okay! Thanks, Judy! Hope you have a good night!" she said.

I turned around. The room was empty. Toni was out. The entire floor was silent.

I was all alone.

I focused on my studies. I started to worry about what was going to happen to me *after* college. What if I got my degree and the board of ed wouldn't let me teach?

I called an organization for advice. It was the American Civil Liberties Union.

"I'm interested in being a teacher," I told the guy who answered the phone. "But I've never met or heard of any teachers who are wheelchair users. Is there anything you suggest I do?"

"Well, just go ahead and take the courses that you need," he responded. "If you have a problem when you graduate, call us."

■ ■ ■

I started to meet other disabled students. We talked a lot about how the university could change to become more accessible. Some people at the university felt like it would be better if we just didn't go to school there at all. There were articles in the paper saying disabled students didn't belong at Long Island University.

The problem was, our parents' generation thought about disability totally differently from how we did. During World War II, America had a president who'd had polio. Franklin Roosevelt used a wheelchair, but the public never saw him in it. He refused to have his picture taken while he was using his wheelchair or being helped in any way. He talked about "beating" his disability and promoted the idea of "curing" disabilities.

We totally disagreed with this. Our disabilities weren't medical problems that we were going to "fix." Our problem was with society. From our perspective, disability was something that could happen to anyone at any time, and frequently did, so it was the right thing for society to expect it and design for it.

We grew up during the civil rights movement. I was eight when Rosa Parks refused to give up her seat in the whites-only section of a bus. I was just starting college when the Civil Rights Act was passed in 1964.

We realized that disabled people not being allowed to attend the same school as the nondisabled kids was also discrimination and segregation.

And isn't it the government's responsibility to make sure all citizens are treated equally?

The more I thought about these issues, the more I got into politics. I ran for student council and won.

■ ■ ■

"No," I said into the telephone. "If we're going to fight the increase in tuition, we have to build more support before we meet with the university leadership."

"I agree," said the student council president. "Let's call a meeting of the full council to strategize."

I clicked the speaker button and hung up the phone.

"Mom! Can you turn me when you have a minute?" I had to take some notes on my conversation with the student council president. I could do that much more easily when I was flipped over.

It was my third year of college and I was lying in my parents' dining room, encased in a body cast from my shoulders to my knees. My hair was cut off, and I had four holes drilled into my head where the doctors had attached a metal crown with four screws. On my cast were two big metal hoops that my parents used to turn me. I'd had two surgeries that were supposed to free me from the braces I wore to hold my body upright and prevent further curvature of my spine. The surgeries fused my spine. But the recovery was long. I was supposed to stay in bed until June. It was only February.

I'd run for junior class secretary the year before and lost. But just after my surgery, the winner quit. I ran again from my spot in the dining room, with some help from my friends, and won. I was on the telephone all the time. Even though I'd been immobilized in a body cast for my entire tenure, I worked really well with the student council president.

Over the past two years, the Vietnam War had accelerated to the point where, as of November of my third year of college, forty thousand Americans were joining the army every month. Lots of them were dying. More of them were coming home wounded. The antiwar movement was spreading, and student activism at Long Island University was growing fast. The student council had been taken over by student activists in the antiwar movement. And I was one of them.

"Thanks, Mom." My mother had come out of the kitchen and rotated me.

It sounds weird—I had holes in my head, a full body cast, and my mom turning me over every couple of hours—but in some ways, my life in the dining room was easier. Not having to constantly worry about asking people for favors was like not having to carry around a two-ton bag of potatoes all the time. I could just do my thing as class secretary, as an equal, alongside everyone else in the "regular" world.

So, all in all, I remember it as a happy time, especially since I was looking forward to my graduation from college, which was just around the corner.

Of course, I had no idea what was about to happen.

CHAPTER FIVE

YOU WANT ME TO WHAT?

Only five steps led up to the brass-plated front doors of the New York City Board of Education, but it could have been two and it wouldn't have mattered. All I knew was that there were steps. So this time, I'd come prepared. I'd recruited my friend Bill.

"Ready?" he asked.

I nodded.

"Here we go!" Bill smiled. He turned me around, grasped the black handles of my wheelchair and pulled me up the stairs backward.

The lobby was vast. Bill pushed my chair to the reception desk. I looked up at the man in uniform behind the counter.

"I'm here to see Dr. James."

"Third floor, number 312. Sign here please." The man sounded bored.

The buttons for the wood-paneled elevator were out of my reach, as usual, which was one of the reasons Bill was there. The elevator was slow and creaky. As I listened to it lumber its way down the shaft from the upper reaches of the building, I thought about the medical exam I was about to go through.

I'd graduated from Long Island University and this medical exam was the last thing standing between me and my teaching license. It was supposed to be routine. A "check the box" kind of thing. All the doctor had to do was determine whether I had any medical issues that would make me a danger to children. Of course, I didn't. But anxiety gripped my stomach. I just knew people had a habit of seeing my wheelchair and thinking *problem*.

The elevator door slid open. Bill pushed me inside and pressed the button for the third floor.

The elevator slogged its way up, past the second floor and stopped. Bill maneuvered my chair out the door and rolled me down the hallway into an office.

"I'm here to see Dr. James," I informed the woman behind the reception desk.

The woman looked up at me. "Judy Heumann?"

"Yes."

"Please wait here." The woman shuffled some papers.

Bill pushed me to the side of the desk and we waited. I could feel myself trembling so I picked up a magazine to try to think about something else.

The door next to the reception opened and an older woman poked her head into the room.

"Judy Heumann?" she called. She had a tight, reserved smile.

"Yes, me." I pushed myself forward.

"I'm Dr. James," she said and ushered me into a small office with a brown wooden desk.

In the beginning, the medical exam seemed predictable. As Dr. James took my blood pressure, listened to my heart, and asked standard questions, I gradually stopped trembling. She asked me questions about the history of my polio and I explained.

Then she got an odd look on her face.

Leaning toward me, she asked me again about my polio-related medical treatment. Her eyes were like nails. I leaned back to try to put some space between us.

What did my medical history from twenty years ago have to do with anything? I thought.

"Raise your arms," she said.

I lifted my forearms up, as far as I could.

Why was she asking about my arms?

"Have you ever walked?" I felt goosebumps rise all over my body. In the back of my head, an alarm clanged.

Something was wrong.

"Well, before my spinal fusion, I used braces and crutches to stand, but I've never really walked," I told her.

She leaned even closer and looked at me with her weird gaze. A cold ball materialized in my stomach.

"Show me how you go to the bathroom," she said.

The question socked me in the gut, like a baseball out of nowhere. I hunched over, trying to breathe.

She couldn't be serious. How was this even possible?

Every single part of me wanted to turn my chair and drive out of the room. As fast as I could.

But I had no choice but to answer.

"Well," my voice cracked, "if other teachers are going to have to show their students how to go to the bathroom then of course I'll do it, but otherwise you can be assured that I can take care of it myself." I sat, stunned at my answer. I'd had no idea what was going to come out of my mouth.

The doctor shifted her eyes away from me.

"Tell me again how you walk," she asked.

I have no idea what I said, but I know it had something to do with what I'd already told her several times. Which is that I don't walk.

My explanation didn't seem to reach her. She wrote something in her folder and snapped it shut. Then she told me to come back for a second appointment with my braces and crutches to show her how I "walked."

The appointment was over.

My chest churned. This was beyond what I'd ever even imagined.

I felt completely and totally alone. She could do or say anything she wanted to me, and there was nothing I could do about it. There were no rules. There were no boundaries.

It was discrimination.

■ ■ ■

In the elevator I told Bill what had happened. But what could he say?

We exited the lobby and he bumped my chair down the steps, as my mind raced on one repeat track: do I give up or keep going?

■ ■ ■

For the follow-up exam I brought extra support.

If I was going to keep going, I wanted a witness. I brought Dr. Theodore Childs. He was head of Long Island University's Disabled Students Program *and* a member of the National Association for the Advancement of Colored People.

But here's what I didn't bring: my crutches or my brace.

Like the last time, Bill dragged my chair up the steps. Again, we sat and waited by the brown couch. When Dr. James poked her head out, I asked if I could bring Dr. Childs into the exam room. But Dr. James refused.

I wheeled into the exam room, where two strange men were waiting. I looked at them, confused. Was I in the wrong room? Who were these men?

Dr. James introduced them as doctors she'd invited to join my medical exam.

What? I thought. Why?

Chilly fingers gripped my stomach and twisted it into knots.

Without saying a word, the three examined me together. Then they asked me about my polio diagnosis, my medical history, and my paralysis.

"When did you get sick?"

"How many surgeries have you had?"

"Have you lived in an institution?"

"Who lives with you?"

"Show us how you walk," one of them said, so close I could feel his breath on my face.

I hesitated. I had to tell them.

"I didn't bring my crutches or my brace," I said.

All three shook their heads and frowned. One of them wrote something on his pad.

I read it upside down. It was one word: "insubordinate."

At one point, Dr. James turned to the men and spoke as if I were invisible. "She wets her pants sometimes."

My mouth fell open.

"What are you talking about?" I whispered.

But she ignored me.

"This," I thought, "is . . . not . . . happening. Not. Possible."

■ ■ ■

Afterward, Bill wheeled me out of the office. I couldn't speak. I felt lacerated, like I'd been lashed with a whip. My mind was filled with one question, and it was this: Am I going to be treated like a disease for my entire life?

All I wanted was to teach second graders.

■ ■ ■

Three months later, the letter arrived in the mail. The New York City Board of Education had determined I was unable to teach.

The reason? "Paralysis of both lower extremities, sequela of poliomyelitis."

Polio.

I was officially a danger to children.

They'd made their decision and printed it on a single white piece of paper.

CHAPTER SIX

THE LAST DROP

There comes a point when a single drop of oil is all that's needed to tip a barrel over—and spark a revolution.

The letter from the board of education was that drop.

I was done. I was done begging for things that everyone else took for granted, done apologizing for my existence.

I was not a disease.

I knew I had to fight the board of ed.

But when I imagined myself sitting in front of everyone, demanding the right to teach, my heart pounded. It pounded so hard, it felt like it was going to explode out of my chest.

I was used to my parents standing up for me. It was very different to think about doing it for myself. I felt like I'd be put under a microscope.

I mean, I'd never actually taught before. I didn't even know if I *could* teach.

How could I publicly stand up and demand the right to do something I had never done before?

Just the thought of it made my body shake.

Everyone would be watching me and wondering, Can a woman in a wheelchair teach?

What if I won and turned out to be a terrible teacher? If I failed, would people think that no one with a disability could teach? I could ruin it for everyone.

But didn't I have just as much right to teach and fail as anyone else?

My friends rallied around me. We'd been expecting that I might be denied my license. My case could be an example. It could raise awareness of our issues. I believed all of this.

Just because you believe something is right, though, doesn't make it any easier to do. It doesn't necessarily stop you from trembling every time you think about doing it.

But if I didn't fight, who would?

CHAPTER SEVEN

ARE YOU
JUDY HEUMANN?

I called the American Civil Liberties Union again.
"I called you two and a half years ago and told
you I wanted to be a teacher," I said to the man on the
phone. I explained what had happened and asked to
make an appointment.

But the man told me I didn't need to come in.

"No," he said. "It's fine. Just give us the information over the phone. Send whatever documents you
have. We'll assess and call you back."

A few days later, the phone rang.

"I'm sorry, Miss Heumann. We've considered your
case and determined that no discrimination has oc-
curred. You've been denied your license for medical
reasons, which is not discrimination."

What? I thought. How the doctor had treated me
wasn't considered discrimination? How could the
denial of my teaching license *not* be discrimination? I
was perfectly mobile in my wheelchair. I could whisk

multiple children to safety on my lap if necessary. Not to mention the fact that I'd passed all my exams.

For years, I'd been counting on the American Civil Liberties Union. The civil rights movement was my friends' and my inspiration. It had helped us to stop blaming ourselves for not being able to walk and start blaming the system. Every time I'd gotten worried about what might happen when I applied for my license, I'd reminded myself that if things went south, there was someone out there who could help me.

But now that someone was telling me that it was my fault.

I racked my brain for a way to convince the man on the phone. The problem was, people didn't associate discrimination with disability. If disability had been included in the Civil Rights Act, I could have quoted the law to him. But instead, I was stuck trying to persuade this man that discrimination against disabled people was even a thing.

I wanted to scream. But I took a deep breath and forced myself to talk calmly.

"Please allow me to come in and speak with you," I said to the man. "I can explain to you how denying me my job on the grounds of a medical condition is, in fact, discriminatory and you can't just write it off as a failed medical exam."

"I'm sorry, Miss Heumann. We've already assessed your case very thoroughly."

I hung up. My veins throbbed.

How was this possible?

Did they just look at me and think *sick*?

Fire spread through my limbs.

I was *never* going to walk again. My friends' bodies were never going to make some dramatic change. This was our reality and it was just fine with us.

These were just facts of life.

It's almost as if the world just doesn't want to accept that people become disabled, I thought. And they're mad at us for simply existing. I'm sorry, but injuries and illnesses and aging are just a part of who we are as humans.

The fire in my chest burned. My jaw clenched.

If this famous organization couldn't understand how what the board of ed did was wrong, then we would have to do it ourselves.

I would blow my story off the map.

■ ■ ■

The first thing I had to do was find a lawyer. The only problem was, I had no clue how to do this. I definitely didn't know any lawyers. The only people I knew were butchers and cops and firefighters. Hmmm, I thought. Maybe I should start somewhere else instead. I also needed publicity. A disabled guy I knew from school was a journalism major and worked for the *New York*

Times. I called him and told him about the board of ed's decision.

■ ■ ■

"Judy! Judy!" my roommate was holding the newspaper in her hand. "There's an article about you being denied the right to teach by the New York City Board of Ed!" she said.

My mouth dropped open. Then I raised my arms and cheered out loud.

The next day, the *New York Times* came out publicly with an editorial expressing support for me.

That afternoon, the phone rang.

"Judy Heumann?" the man said. "My name is Roy Lucas. I'm a lawyer and I'm working on some civil rights research. I read about your situation in the paper and I'd like to interview you for the project."

Wait, what? I thought. A lawyer calling *me*? I couldn't process it.

"Yes," I said, after a few minutes of gaping silence. "I'd be happy to be interviewed."

So he asked me a bunch of questions, and I decided to ask him a bunch of questions. At the end of the call, I asked if he'd be willing to represent me in a case against the board of ed.

He agreed.

When I hung up, I stared at the phone. Did that really just happen?

I put my hand over my heart. Thank you, I whispered.

■ ■ ■

The next day, one of my father's regular customers came into my dad's butcher shop to buy a steak. It was Arthur Schwartzbart, who also happened to be a lawyer. My dad told him about my situation and asked if he'd be willing to help represent me.

Overnight, I had a team of lawyers.

■ ■ ■

Then, weirdly, I became kind of famous.

The newspapers couldn't get enough of my story. Article after article came out.

"You Can Be President, Not Teacher, with Polio," one headline read.

Getting interviewed over and over again pushed me into the water at the deep end. I had no experience with public speaking. So I channeled my dad and pretended the reporter was sitting at our kitchen table, having dinner with us. My dad loved to have big conversations about politics at dinner. The only thing my dad liked more than having big conversations about politics at the dinner table was teaching us how to have big conversations about politics at the dinner table.

"Be bold," he always told us. "Interrupt."

His mantra was: "Do whatever you have to do to get your point across and know your facts."

■ ■ ■

I got letters from all over the country. Some congress-women in Washington, DC, wrote to the mayor of New York City, asking why the board of ed wouldn't let me teach. And the teachers' union came out and publicly supported me.

People started recognizing me in public. I'd finally gotten a motorized wheelchair! Which meant I could go to all kinds of places by myself. As I wheeled down the street, people would stop me to tell me their stories.

"I've experienced discrimination too," one man said.

"My disabled father was unemployed my whole life," another woman told me.

"My sister isn't allowed into school," a boy said to me.

I went whole hog with the media.

"We're not going to let a hypocritical society give us a token education and then bury us," I told one reporter. I had fully taken on my dad's dinner table lessons. I wouldn't let anyone cut me off. I refused to back down.

It all felt amazing, but to tell the truth, I also felt awkward. Because, yes, I did want my story to be told, but I wasn't used to so much attention. I didn't want it to be all about me. I felt like my fight represented a bigger issue than just my teaching license.

Maybe I'd get a job, but what I really wanted was to show people there was absolutely no reason why wheelchair users couldn't be teachers. Actually, I wanted to show people there was absolutely no reason why anyone with any type of disability couldn't be whatever they wanted to be.

■ ■ ■

Then, the phone rang again. It was a producer from *The Today Show*.

"We want to invite you to be on the show," the woman told me.

What? I thought. *The Today Show*? As in, *the actual Today Show*?

That is what I wanted to say.

But this is what I did say: "That would be great, thank you."

They wanted to set up a debate between me and this guy in government named Bob Hermann, who dealt with special education. It would be my first chance to confront the government on national television.

The next morning, I woke up in a cold sweat. I couldn't go on TV and debate this government official. Who was I to think that I knew better than this older man? I was only twenty-two and he'd probably been working in government since I was little.

I just couldn't do it. That day, I rolled around feeling like fingers were squeezing my heart. I could barely breathe.

Okay, I thought. I have got to get it together. I have got to do this no matter what.

I may have no idea what I'm doing, but I'm going to do it anyway.

■ ■ ■

And, boy, did I do it.

Poor Bob Hermann. I went after him like a dog with a bone.

It was no longer about me.

It was about everyone like me. Every one of my friends from Health Conservation 21. Every one of my friends from camp. Everyone who had a disability. Anyone who'd ever been locked up or ignored. It was about how no one was listening to us, and nothing was happening.

I felt like we finally had an opportunity to get people to listen and make things right.

Yes, I did want to be a teacher, but it was much, much more than that.

■ ■ ■

Then, the next thing I knew, it was the day of the court hearing.

CHAPTER EIGHT

THE FIGHT

I wheeled into the courtroom, flanked by my team: my lawyers, my parents, and my brothers. I braked my chair right in front of the judge's podium, which was empty.

When the judge entered, I couldn't take my eyes off her. Judge Constance Baker Motley was tall and stately. But it wasn't her looks. It was her presence. She was godlike.

Judge Constance Baker Motley was the first Black female judge ever to be appointed to federal court. Before she became a judge, she'd been a famous fighter for civil rights who defended protesters in the civil rights movement.

Wow! Wow! Wow! I thought. This is *incredible*.

All my friends had also shown up. They were rowdy, waving at me and wheeling into the back rows.

I thought back to my phone call to the American Civil Liberties Union. I'd been so hurt and angry after they turned me down. And now, here I was.

I was bringing a disability civil rights lawsuit against the New York City Board of Education *and* my judge was a famous civil rights leader.

Sometimes a door just slides open when you least expect it.

■ ■ ■

Judge Baker Motley listened to our lawyers. Watching her face, my heart was in my mouth. It was impossible to tell what she was thinking.

Then she spoke. Her voice was very soft.

I leaned forward to hear her.

"You should make no mistake about my interest in this case," she said to the representatives from the board of ed. The courtroom was dead quiet. Her words dropped like steel pellets. "I suggest that you do whatever you need to do to resolve this problem."

My heart jumped.

Her meaning was clear: fix this situation now.

I looked at the board of ed representatives and their lawyer. They were whispering among themselves. The lawyer stood.

"Ma'am, we stand down."

What? They weren't going to argue? I thought.

They must have never expected me to fight back.

My mouth curled into an enormous Cheshire cat grin.

It was over.

And we had won.

■ ■ ■

The doctor at my third medical exam was very different from Dr. James.

"I'm sorry," she said. "This never should have happened." The doctor sounded like she was apologizing for all ableist doctors ever.

"You're right about that," I said. "But thank you." She filled out some forms, wished me luck, and sent me off.

I had my teaching license.

Now the perfect ending to this story would go something along the lines of, "so then I got my license, found a job, and lived happily ever after." But that's not how it went, because I couldn't get a job, and then lots of other things happened.

First, no one would hire me.

So we had to call the papers back and a whole new round of articles came out. After that, the principal at my old school offered me a job and I went back to Health Conservation 21.

■ ■ ■

On the first day of school, I drove my chair up the new ramp. I tried to look serious. I was "Miss Heumann"

Me officially being a teacher

now, and I had a class of the "kids upstairs" to teach.

But light bubbled inside me and I couldn't stop smiling.

■ ■ ■

At that time, lots of people still recognized me in public. They'd be driving down the street and stop, honk their horns, and beckon me over to say hello. They came up to me in stores and stopped me on the sidewalk. Some of them just wanted to say, "Congratulations! Keep it up." But most of them wanted to tell me more stories about their own experiences of discrimination.

It made me think. I was so close to not fighting. What if I *hadn't* fought? What if I'd just let it go because I didn't want to make a fuss?

The thing is, I was really afraid of losing the court case, but even if I'd lost, just doing it would have changed my life. Because it made me speak up and tell the system it was wrong—about me and about everybody else.

A little while later, the state of New York passed a law to ensure that people who were blind or physically disabled would not be prevented from teaching.

But we were just getting started.

CHAPTER NINE

AM I READING CORRECTLY?

I was at my desk in my bedroom. In front of me were pages and pages of legislation that Rehab had proposed that the House of Representatives and the Senate, otherwise known as Congress, make into laws.

Here's where you might be wondering: What *is* legislation and why are you reading it?

Well, the House of Representatives and the Senate, as you may know, are in charge of making laws—and legislation is just what they call the laws that they're either thinking about passing or have already passed and made official.

So, yes, I was spending my Saturdays reading potential laws. Exciting, I know. But these were laws that, if they got passed, would affect disabled people. Which meant, these laws could change our lives.

I rubbed my eyes. Reading hours of government documents can make you very sleepy.

Then, out of the corner of my eye, I saw something funny. Was I reading it correctly?

I read the sentence again.

Whoa. I *was* reading correctly.

I read it over and over again. It was Section 504 of the proposed law.

No otherwise qualified handicapped individual in the United States, as defined in section 7(6), shall, solely by reason of his handicap, be excluded from the participation in, be denied the benefits of, or be subjected to discrimination under any program or activity receiving Federal financial assistance.

No. Way.

This sentence actually acknowledged that discrimination against disabled people *existed*. *And* made it illegal.

Really?

I was wide awake now.

I began to imagine how this law could affect us. It wouldn't make discrimination illegal everywhere—only in those places that got money from the federal government. But that could include so much, like education and transportation and work.

It could be a beginning.

■ ■ ■

I called my fellow members from Disabled in Action. In the aftermath of the lawsuit, we'd used my exposure from the media to get all kinds of disabled people together to start an organization—it was called Disabled in Action. I told them what I'd read.

"It's under Section 504 of the legislation." I swear the phone line was vibrating we were so excited.

The thing is, we could bring a lawsuit anytime that anyone was unfair and excluded us, like I did against the New York City Board of Education. But winning that lawsuit was kind of a crapshoot. I was lucky, for example, that I'd gotten a civil rights leader as my judge. There were tons of judges who would have sided with the board of ed against me because we didn't have laws that said discrimination was a thing that happened to disabled people.

Which is why this legislation was so important.

Basically, this one sentence was the difference between us going into battle empty-handed and us going into battle with a meat ax.

That one sentence was our weapon for winning the war on discrimination.

If we could get this passed, we could take the whole thing down.

■ ■ ■

It started with a one-two punch.

Congress voted to pass Section 504.

And then President Nixon vetoed it.

■ ■ ■

We planned a series of events to protest the veto. We rolled ourselves, for example, into Manhattan traffic at rush hour. The commuters were *not* happy. People beeped their horns and yelled at us to get out of the road. The problem was, there weren't enough of us. We looked like a small group of lost people in traffic, not a major group of activists.

It was hard to get people to our protests. The trains weren't accessible and there were only a few buses built for wheelchairs. Plus, all the disabled people in New York City were like me: patching their life together with favors. It's hard to go to protests when you're not sure how or where you're going to go to the bathroom.

We recruited some Vietnam vets who'd returned from the war unable to walk and with other disabilities. There were a lot of them and they were angry. They'd fought a war and risked their lives and then they'd come home to a country where they now couldn't go to the store without someone bumping them off the curbs.

The vets marched through Times Square with us to Nixon's headquarters.

"I've finally met someone crazier than me," one of them said to me.

■ ■ ■

But the government continued to ignore us.

Then, because Nixon had vetoed it, the legislation that Section 504 was a part of got kicked back to Congress to start through the whole process again.

It was time to regroup.

■ ■ ■

Not too long after our series of protests to get the law signed, the phone rang. I answered it at my desk in my bedroom. It was a stranger.

"Judy," the man said, as if he knew me. "This is Ed Roberts. I am calling from Berkeley, California. I've heard a lot about you. I want you to move here. I'm recruiting leaders who can be a part of what we're doing."

"What?" I said. I'd vaguely heard of Ed Roberts, but this was surreal.

"I had polio when I was fourteen," he told me. "I can only use two fingers and I can't breathe on my own for very long. I was the first person with a major disability to go to the University of California in Berkeley and I've started an organization out here called the Center for Independent Living."

The University of California, Ed told me, had refused to allow him to live at school. He'd had to fight. Eventually, university officials had agreed to let him live on campus, but because he used an iron lung—a massive machine that breathes for him—he was forced to live all by himself in an empty wing of the hospital.

"Which was pretty lonely at first," Ed chuckled, "until a bunch of other disabled kids started school and moved in with me. We called ourselves the Rolling Quads."

Because Ed and the Rolling Quads were continually having to solve problems, like fixing their wheelchairs and figuring out how to get to places, they ended up starting an organization to help themselves and all the other disabled people around campus. This is what they called the Center for Independent Living, the first organization to ever help disabled people live on their own.

"It sounds awesome, Ed. But, honestly, I can't leave New York!" I said. "Between the support of my family and paying my roommates to help me get up and dressed, go to bed at night, and go to the bathroom, I've cobbled together a support system that lets me live in my own apartment. If I left my roommates and my family, how would I live?"

"But Judy, this is exactly the point!" Ed told me. "California provides funding for disabled people to hire personal assistance, so you don't *have* to depend on roommates and friends like you do in New York. I live without depending on my family or roommates at all!"

This was hard to process. Ed, who could only move two fingers, *that* Ed—didn't depend on his roommates? Or his family? California actually helped disabled people live independently?

I told my friend Nancy Di'Angelo that I was thinking of moving to California. She said she wanted to come too. It was all I needed to push me over the edge.

I decided.

California, here we come.

■　■　■

Ed and some of the people from the Center for Independent Living helped us move. They found us an apartment and had someone meet us at the airport. The next day, we applied to the state of California for funding to pay for our personal assistance.

When we got approved, Nancy and I danced up and down the living room. I couldn't wait to interview and hire someone to help me. Having someone whose actual job it was to help me get up and go to bed at night? Amazing. It would mean that I didn't have to spend my day obsessing about the logistics of my life.

It would be the end of my Rubik's Cube of favors.

．　．　．

The woman I hired as my personal attendant was about my age and nice.

On her first day, she came to help me get out of bed and get dressed. That night she came back to help me get into bed. As she was leaving, she paused.

"What time do you want to get up tomorrow, Judy?" she asked, waiting by the door for me to answer.

Well, you could have knocked me over with a ball of scrunchies. Never in my life had someone asked me what time I wanted to get out of bed. It was never a question of what *I* wanted. It was what was convenient for my roommate or my random friend across the hall or my mother.

For the first time in my life, I had the amazing and incredible ability to get up when *I* wanted.

．　．　．

Nancy and I shared an apartment near the university. The Center for Independent Living was in the same building, which meant people were constantly coming

Me and Ed Roberts

and going. Disabled people were coming to California from all over the country to be a part of what Ed and everyone was doing. I made friends everywhere. Berkeley was small and was installing ramps on the streets and doing other things to make the city accessible. A lot of my new friends had wheelchair accessible vans they could drive so we could go places by ourselves. I could go to parties, friends' houses, and out to dinner without having to worry about the logistics.

Even more importantly, because all of us could get around so much more easily, we could get more involved in politics and organize more protests.

Which meant that we could stick to Section 504 like wasps on a triple-berry smoothie. Believe it or not, it took a few years for 504 to wind its way through the political system, as it moved one slow step after another.

Until the day it stopped.

PART TWO

THREE
YEARS
LATER

CHAPTER TEN

WEIRD SLEEPOVER

I handed my underwear and toothbrush to my personal attendant.

"Do you mind putting these in my bag for me?" I turned my wheelchair around so she could reach my backpack. She was helping me get ready for the day.

"Going somewhere?" she asked me, putting my toothbrush and underwear into my backpack. She knew it wasn't normal for me to pack an extra set of undergarments for a day at the office.

"The protest may go a little long today," I said, putting on my big silver-rimmed glasses as she zipped my jacket. If things went like we predicted, there was a possibility I might not be home for several days.

I could get detained.

■ ■ ■

I drove my wheelchair onto the sidewalk in front of my house. The morning fog was chilly. I looked up and down the street. A van from the Center for

Independent Living, was supposed to pick me up and take me into San Francisco, but I was early. I spent the time reviewing my plan.

Congress had, not too long ago, finally passed Section 504 again. This, of course, was exactly what we wanted, but we had a problem. Our problem was that Section 504 would only become useful when the secretary of the Department of Health, Education, and Welfare (HEW) signed something called the "enabling regulations," which are rules that explain how a law should work and be enforced.

To cut to the chase, if the enabling regulations for Section 504 didn't get signed, the law would basically never mean anything to anybody.

Joseph Califano was the head of Health, Education, and Welfare, which meant he was the guy in charge of signing the regulations. But he wasn't doing it. In fact, he was delaying the signing. Even worse, he was actually trying to *change* the regulations. Why? Because all the companies that would be affected by the law were putting pressure on him to weaken it.

So guess who Mr. Califano was listening to. Big corporations.

Guess who he was *not* listening to. Us.

We, the activists, had tried everything to get him to sign the regulations. Sometimes we had tried to be helpful. Other times we had protested. But no matter what we said or did, Califano continued to ignore us.

So we made a decision. We told the government that if the regulations were not signed by April 5, we would take our protests up a notch. A big notch.

Today was April 5.

■ ■ ■

"Hey! How's it going? Ready?"

I was so deep in my thoughts, I hadn't noticed the staffer from the Center for Independent Living pulling up in the van.

I drove my wheelchair onto the van's lift. We headed down the street.

Our plan was to have a day of massive simultaneous protests at the Health, Education, and Welfare offices across the country—Washington, DC, Atlanta, Boston, New York City, Los Angeles, Denver, Chicago, Dallas, Philadelphia, and San Francisco.

Kitty Cone and I were part of the Committee to Save 504, and we were in charge of organizing the San Francisco event.

Kitty, who had muscular dystrophy and used a wheelchair, was a community organizer extraordinaire. We'd worked on the event for months, making flyers, calling people, organizing committees to do various jobs. We regularly worked until the wee hours of the morning and ended up doing everything together, like an old married couple. We were like the Dunphys on

Modern Family—I was the mom, who always thought she was right, and Kitty was like the dad and constantly making people laugh.

But as we got closer and closer to April 5, we started to get worried. Not about whether people would show up at our protest, but more about whether it would actually work. Would the government really listen to us?

We had our doubts. We'd both been ignored many, many times in our lives and we knew how it worked.

So, secretly, Kitty and I had decided to take the San Francisco protest just one little step further than the others.

Which is why I had an extra set of undies in my backpack.

■ ■ ■

We crossed the Bay Bridge, and the buildings of San Francisco emerged out of the fog. Taking the second exit off the freeway, suddenly we were in the middle of the city. All around us people were walking down the sidewalk, chatting, waiting at traffic lights, crossing streets—stepping up, down, and over the curbs, without even noticing what they were doing. Ugh, I thought. Curbs and steps are the bane of my life.

We pulled into a parking spot across the street from the San Francisco Federal Building, which is where the

San Francisco office of Health, Education, and Welfare was. The front of the building faced a large plaza, where three ornate archways curved over the main entrance.

■　■　■

Preparations for the protest were already in motion. Dead center in front of the San Francisco Federal Building sat Kitty in her wheelchair. She was wheeling around and shouting orders at a group of people assembling a stage.

Next to the stage, two men took a microphone and sound system out of the back of a van and walked over to a woman setting up a table. A deaf staffer from the Center for Independent Living was supervising, speaking in rapid sign language with the sound guys while a sign language interpreter stood translating next to him. Meanwhile, ten or so other people hurried back and forth across the plaza, carrying things, setting things up, and talking. A couple of people walked with white canes, another spoke in sign language with an interpreter, and the rest were in wheelchairs. My boyfriend, Jim, walked by in his aviator sunglasses, talking to a woman who was blind.

Kitty caught my eye from across the plaza, and beckoned me to come over. As I wheeled toward her, a group of people rounded the corner of the building, and six others in wheelchairs poured from a van parked on the street. Our event was going to be big. I just knew it.

■ ■ ■

It was a perfect sunny day. To kick things off, a bunch of speakers talked about Section 504 and why it mattered. The crowd loved it. They applauded uproariously after each speaker—the hearing people clapped, and the deaf people raised their hands and shook them in front of their faces, which is the sign language version of clapping. An interpreter stood on the stage, translating each speaker into sign language.

Kitty was positioned in front of the microphone, finishing her speech. "Sign 504! Sign 504! Sign 504!" she chanted. The crowd, which seemed to be growing, clapped and chanted, waving their hands in the air.

It was my turn to speak.

I drove my chair forward to the microphone. My heart pounded.

The crowd cheered. I sat a moment and waited. Hundreds of faces looked at me.

■ ■ ■

"When I was five years old, I was denied the right to go to school. When I was finally allowed to start school in the fourth grade, some of my classmates were eighteen years old and still didn't know how to read.

"When they are signed, the regulations for Section 504 will be a historic and monumental first step toward knocking down the walls that stop us, people with disabilities, from being full and equal participants in society.

"For the past few years," I went on, and suddenly I got choked up. I paused and looked down. The crowd was utterly silent. "We have played by the rules." I took a breath, trying to get ahold of myself.

"We created the American Coalition for Citizens with Disabilities. We attended meetings in Washington, commented on drafts of the regulations, and spoke with institutions all over the country. We were told Jimmy Carter's administration would sign the regulations, unchanged. We believed him.

"Now Secretary Califano is dragging his feet. We have no reason to trust him. We are here to say *enough is enough*.

"For too long, we have believed that if we played by the rules and did what we were told, we would be included in the American Dream.

"We have waited too long, made too many compromises, and been too patient.

"We will no longer be patient. There will be no more compromise.

"We will accept no more discrimination."

Me

For one split second I gazed out at the crowd and then raised my hand.

"Sign 504! Sign 504! Sign 504!" I chanted.

The crowd thundered. They chanted and shouted, raised their hands and shook them. I chanted with them for a minute and then turned to wheel to the back of the stage. Ed Roberts was already behind me.

"That was great," he grinned.

I grinned back.

■ ■ ■

Ed's wheelchair reclined to the point where it was almost horizontal. His attendant held the microphone in front of his face. This is what I recall Ed saying:

"When I was fourteen, I had polio. While I was sick, the doctor said to my mother, 'You should hope he dies because if he survives, his brain won't work. He will be a vegetable.'

"When I recovered, my life had changed. For a long time, I wanted to die. I stopped eating to try to

kill myself. And then I realized I didn't want to die."
Ed was handsome as usual, the breeze ruffled his
brown hair. He was out of his iron lung and using a
frog-breathing technique, gulping air into his lungs
after every few words. Next to him stood the sign language interpreter, his hands moving.

"So I come before you now as an artichoke. Prickly
on the outside with a big heart on the inside. When you
see me, I hope you see what is possible, where others
saw only what was not possible.

"And I tell you this. Our whole lives we are told
what we can and cannot do. But know this now: what
we are trying to do here is possible.

"Only *we* decide what is right for us."

■ ■ ■

The plaza was hanging on his every word.

"So what do we want?" he shouted.

Cheers exploded and then chanting.

"Sign 504! Sign 504! Sign 504!"

Then our final presenter climbed onto the stage,
guitar in hand. His black hair glistened. He started to
sing. The crowd swayed in unison.

"Keep your eyes on the prize, hold on, hold on,"
the crowd joined in, singing out loud. Deaf people
signed. People linked hands. The guitar player was
blind, but I'm sure he could feel the pulsating energy.

Taking a second or two to let the atmosphere sweep over me, I slowly moved my chair. It was almost time for me to say the words Kitty and I had agreed on.

The song ended. A silence crystallized. Grace reigned over the quiet plaza.

Softly, I shifted to be in front of the microphone. Then, before anyone could move, I leaned up and yelled.

"Let's go and tell HEW the federal government cannot steal our civil rights!"

I turned and headed for the door of the federal building.

■ ■ ■

It was instant mayhem.

People surged behind me. Those who could walk went up the steps. Blind people pushed people in manual wheelchairs, the person in the wheelchair navigating. The people in electric chairs drove themselves up a ramp to the right of the stairs.

Inside, the lobby of the building was mobbed. Someone pushed the button for the elevator. Immediately, it was crammed with people.

The elevator rose swiftly, past the first floor to the fourth floor. Wheeling out, people gushed into the hallway. The area teemed with people pushing chairs, leaning on crutches, holding white canes.

Moving quickly but carefully, I wheeled down the hall and came to an office door marked Regional Director, Federal Department of Health, Education, and Welfare. A deaf man opened the door for me, standing slightly to the side so I could squeeze my chair through the narrow doorway. I rolled up to the receptionist, who was sitting behind a white desk.

"We have a meeting with Joe Maldonado," I said to the woman. She looked alarmed.

Kitty came up behind me.

"Wow!"

"Yeah, I never thought we'd get this many people."

Taking our names, the receptionist backed apprehensively away from us toward a door to her left. Behind us, more people spilled into the lobby, sitting in their wheelchairs, leaning against walls.

The receptionist came back.

"Mr. Maldonado will see you now. This way, please."

Kitty and I followed her down the hallway, but then I paused and turned back.

"Come with us," I said to a bunch of protesters in the reception area and gestured for them to follow. A considerable group trailed us into Maldonado's office.

■ ■ ■

Joe Maldonado was a small man with graying, curly hair. When we entered the room, he stood up and awkwardly motioned for us to sit, seeming not to process that many of us already were.

"What can I do for you?" Joe Maldonado asked, clearly shocked at the sight of us.

"We're here to ask about the status of the enabling regulations for Section 504," I said loudly.

Maldonado leaned back uneasily in his chair, with a guarded look. His light-colored suit was tight across his shoulders, a white polka-dot tie rested on his chest. Behind me, more demonstrators packed themselves into the office.

The room hushed with attention.

"What is Section 504?" he asked.

I paused. What? Was he serious?

"Section 504 of Title V of the 1973 Rehabilitation Act prohibits discrimination against people with disabilities in institutions and programs receiving federal funding. The Department of Health, Education, and Welfare is responsible for finalizing the enabling regulations for it. Do you know anything at all about what's happening with these regulations in Washington?" I hoped my voice was echoing down the hall to the rest of the protesters.

"I'm sorry, I don't know anything about Section 504 or about what is happening with these regulations," Maldonado said again, turning red.

Several worried wrinkles appeared on his forehead.

"Can we please speak with the staff on your team who work on 504?" I asked.

Maldonado looked displeased. "I am telling you, we don't have any information for you."

"I understand," I said, "but we'd like to speak with your staff, please."

For a minute, Maldonado looked like he was going to refuse. Then he walked out and came back a moment later with two men. I asked them about the regulations.

They looked utterly blank.

I explained again. Exasperation slipped into my voice. The sign language interpreter stood behind me, interpreting for the rest of the protesters.

The entire floor watched and listened.

But it was true. Neither Maldonado nor his staff had any clue what I was talking about.

Hot lava consumed my body.

This might just be a *job* to Maldonado, but his job affected us—every single person currently in his office and millions more. Did he not understand that?

Lava turned to ice, as I coldly bombarded Maldonado with question after question, asking why they were watering down the regulations, what changes were being proposed, why the department wasn't involving the community in the changes, and when the regulations were coming out.

Maldonado looked like he was trying to disappear under his desk.

I refused to feel sorry for him. I leaned forward.

My heart throbbed.

Now. Do it now, I thought.

I looked straight into Maldonado's eyes.

"Section 504 is critical for our lives," I said. Behind me, the crowd held its breath.

"We're not leaving until we get assurances." The words came from some wellspring within me. My heart slowed to a steady beat. My body felt joined with the earth.

"You don't care. You don't care," the crowd chanted behind me.

Maldonado looked at us. Maybe he looked at us and saw a room full of people who would give in if he stared us down long enough. But then he got up and walked out of the office.

Kitty and I looked at each other. I leaned over and whispered.

"How did I do?" I felt like I'd had an out-of-body experience.

"You made mincemeat out of him," Kitty laughed.

Later I learned that while we were with Maldonado, three female HEW employees had been walking around, offering the protesters in the lobby lemonade and cookies. Like we were on some kind of field trip.

Evidently, they'd under-catered.

CHAPTER ELEVEN

AND SUDDENLY, WE'RE VISIBLE

As soon as Maldonado and the rest of the staff left for the night, Kitty and I gathered everyone in the main reception area of the office. It was a critical moment, but I was completely unprepared with any kind of speech. I had no choice. I just had to be totally honest.

"We need you to stay with us in the building until the government signs the regulations for 504!" I told the crowd. "Please consider staying."

No one spoke. I waited, my heart in my throat.

For people with disabilities, a sleepover is not an easy thing. We can't just grab some sandwiches and a toothbrush and call it a day. In addition to the help we might need to pee, a pretty high number of us also require various types of daily medications and have things like catheters that need to be changed, or we need to get turned at night to avoid getting bedsores. Many people, of course, had come to the protest without a personal attendant or food or anything.

If ten people stay, it will be a miracle, I thought.

But then, one by one, hands slowly went up. Some people yelled.

"Yes! We can do it!" And, "Stay!"

Thankfully, a few personal attendants and a sign language interpreter also raised their hands.

In the end, seventy-five people committed to staying. I was dizzy. Seventy-five? It was way beyond what I'd hoped for.

Kitty and I went to Maldonado's office to regroup, along with my boyfriend, Jim, and several of our key people from the Center for Independent Living.

We looked at each other. What next?

"We have to figure out how we're going to feed everyone," Kitty said.

"I wonder what's happening with the other protests," Jim chimed in.

"We better come up with a plan for the press," I added.

Meanwhile, in the rest of the office, the protesters introduced themselves to each other and spread out to explore the space. The offices were small, with large windows and a few couches and rugs scattered here and there. There was a good-sized conference room with an orange shag rug, which people immediately took over. Sitting around the conference table, they pulled candy bars and snacks out of their backpacks to share.

■ ■ ■

We had to find out what was happening with the protesters in the other cities. We got on Maldonado's phone
and made calls. It turned out that those in DC, Denver,
and LA had also refused to leave. There were about fifty
protesters in DC, seven in Denver, and twenty in LA.

Which meant we were, at that very moment, occu-
pying not one, not two, but *four* federal buildings.

The DC group told us what had happened with
Califano.

"He was on a trip and rushed back to DC just to
meet with us," they said.

"Well, now we know how to get Califano's attention," Kitty laughed. "Just threaten to sleep over in his
office."

"Then he stood on top of a coffee table and an-
nounced that he *was* planning to sign the regulations.
He just needed a little longer to study them," they
told us.

Kitty burst out.

"He actually said he was going to *study* them?"

"Unbelievable," I said.

"He is still not getting this," said Pat Wright, one
of my friends who had joined the protest. Pushing her
blond hair off her face, Pat was always matter-of-fact.

For the last three years, the regulations had been
studied, commented on, and revised over and over

again. If Califano was still talking about studying them, especially without our participation, then he clearly had no intention of paying any attention to us. If I'd had any doubts about what we were doing, they disappeared at that moment.

I was so sick and tired of people making decisions that affected our lives without talking to us that I could vomit.

"Now we're alone in the office," the DC protesters continued, "but Califano's got us guarded. We're not allowed to come or go and no one's allowed to bring us food. All we've had is a glass of water and a donut for five hours."

My group in San Francisco looked at each other. I knew what they were thinking.

Califano was going to try to starve them out.

"Hang in there as long as you can," I said.

■ ■ ■

We had to figure out how we were going to take care of the protesters in San Francisco. The security guards had locked the doors to the building to keep anyone else from getting in and adding to our numbers. The problem with that was, we would need food and access to medications—and soon. We would also need a way to reach out to people and the press.

I mean, you can't just take over a federal building and then not tell anyone why you did it. If you're making a point, you have to make it. Preferably in the newspaper.

■ ■ ■

How many committees do you need to support a large group of disabled people living in an office for an indefinite period of time? We created one committee for food, one for medications, one for press, and one for outreach—because we had to stay in touch with all the other civil rights groups so they would support us. We also added one for recreation. With this many people in an enclosed space, we'd definitely need things to do.

We decided to designate a few people as official conduits of communication between us and the security guards. We made them armbands to wear and called them the monitors.

Kitty taped a cardboard box over the air conditioner in Maldonado's office and created a makeshift refrigerator to keep medications cold.

To deal with food right away, we called two of our allies—the Delancey Street Foundation, a rehabilitation program for drug addicts and ex-convicts, and the Salvation Army—to see if they might be willing to bring us meals for the next day. They agreed and my heart rate slowed down, almost back to normal.

At three in the morning, we emerged from Maldonado's office. The protesters had found a way to sleep. They were sprawled across the floor, head to toe. A few of the personal attendants were waking up to turn people. Looking for a place to bed down for the few hours left of the night, Jim and I ended up sleeping in a freight elevator. Kitty slept in a closet.

■   ■   ■

The next morning, I woke with a start.

Where was I?

The feeling of hard floor beneath me reminded me. I looked over at Jim; he was still sleeping. I checked my watch. Six in the morning. I'd slept three hours.

I poked Jim. I wanted to get up so we could find out what the press had said about us.

■   ■   ■

"An Occupation Army of Cripples Has Taken over the San Francisco Federal Building," read one headline. Jim and I, and Kitty, Pat, and a few others were gathered around a newspaper on Maldonado's desk. The little television in Maldonado's office was on. Our sit-in was all over the San Francisco newspapers, television, and radio.

"It all started this morning here at the old Federal Building at 50 Fulton Street when an incident took place outside. Immediately after that demonstration this morning, the handicapped started invading the building," a television segment reported.

"They're talking about us like we're a foreign army," I said. "People aren't used to thinking of us as fighters. When they think about us at all," I added. "Normally we're so invisible."

I mean, think about it. If people didn't see us at school (because we weren't allowed in), or at their place of employment (because we couldn't physically access it or because we couldn't get hired), or in restaurants or theaters, then where would they have seen us?

Well, I'll hazard a guess. At that time, the most likely place they would have seen us would have been on television. At that time, there were these shows called telethons, where celebrities raised money on TV for children with muscular dystrophy and cerebral palsy. The way these telethons worked was by trotting out a sick-looking child with the express purpose of inspiring people's sympathy. So that meant people associated these sick, pitiful images with us.

Basically, we were the kind of people you felt sorry for and raised money to cure. Not the kind of people who fought back.

Well, I thought, that was about to change!

It was time to share our side of the story.

We sent out an announcement that we'd be holding a press conference that afternoon.

■ ■ ■

The first thing we did was educate the reporters about terminology.

"Do not use the terms 'crippled' or 'handicapped,' 'mute' or 'dumb,'" we said. "We are none of these things. We are disabled people and this is our position on Section 504." The reporters scribbled on their pads. Television cameras rolled.

What a pleasure it was to be able to teach them about how discrimination worked and our civil rights.

"Quite frankly," I told one reporter from a national television station, "I think it's going to be very difficult for them to put a lot of pressure on us. When we asked them yesterday if they'd read 504, every single one of the people in that office said no. They should thank us for being here and welcome the opportunity that, finally, they're going to get educated about the law that they're supposed to be enforcing."

After the press conference, we got a message from HEW.

"The DC protesters have left," Kitty said, holding a piece of paper in her hand.

"What? No!" I grabbed it and read it out loud to the group. It was a statement from Califano.

"The demonstration by the handicapped that ended this afternoon underscores the legitimate claim that this group has made on the American conscience. They have suffered discrimination that is wholly unjust. The 504 regulations that I will sign next month will, I believe, be a significant step toward remedying past injustices suffered by the handicapped citizens in helping them achieve the independence, dignity, and fair treatment, which is theirs by right."

"Bologna." Pat said at my elbow.

We called the DC protesters to get the real story.

"We stayed as long as we could," they said. "We had no food. They wouldn't let anyone bring us anything."

A tsunami rolled through my body.

Califano had *deliberately* starved them out and was now *pretending* to be supportive of the cause. He couldn't risk appearing mean toward "sick and pitiful" people, so he was faking it. I bet he assumed that if he reassured the public that he was taking "reasonable steps" in the face of our "craziness," the public would forget about us.

"That's it," said one of the protesters who was listening. "I'm not eating until Califano signs the regulations."

"Me neither," I said, without thinking. "A true democracy wants its citizens to make sure its government is fair." I was too angry to be hungry anyway.

But now we had a problem. We were only in our first full day of occupation and DC had already fizzled. New York was down to ten people, Denver was hanging on by a thread, and the Los Angeles protest was in single digits. Califano was going to think we were all going to cave in.

■ ■ ■

We called a meeting of all the protesters.

"The DC protesters have left and we're losing momentum all over the country," I said. "Califano thinks that if he just waits, we'll fold. We have to prove him wrong. Even more than before, we need to stay in our position and hold strong. If we give up and lose this building, we lose our only negotiating chip." I paused. We couldn't ask people to stay indefinitely. That would be overwhelming. We could only ask people to commit to one day at a time.

"Can you stay one more night? Just one night will make a difference."

Again, one by one, the protesters volunteered.

There were 110 people.

We'd grown by thirty-five.

CHAPTER TWELVE

DINNER TONIGHT COURTESY OF THE BLACK PANTHERS

"Judy! Judy! Wake up!"

I opened one eye. A shot of adrenaline spiked through my body. A monitor was standing in front of me, a serious look on his face.

"What's happening?" I looked at my watch. It was six in the morning. Next to me, Jim sat up.

"The security guards aren't allowing anyone into the building. People can leave, but they can't come back in. Nobody can come back in. Judy, I think they've been ordered to completely shut down the building."

I looked at Jim and then back at the monitor.

It was Easter weekend, which meant that people would want to go home to see their kids. Not to mention the fact that this also meant no food, no medications, no change of clothes could be brought in—nothing.

"People are going to start leaving," I said.

Jim and I went to assess the damage.

The hot water in the bathrooms was shut off. The office phone lines had been blocked for outgoing calls. Our only means of calling the outside world was two pay phones in the hallway.

Califano was squeezing us out.

We listened to the news.

"By now this demonstration here in San Francisco is clearly symbolic," said one reporter. "The group which left the Washington DC offices of HEW yesterday afternoon were the only ones who really had direct access to Secretary Joseph Califano. Any demonstration here in San Francisco, well, can only be to show support. But it can't do anything tangible to get that anti-discrimination law signed right now."

We were being dismissed. Again.

And the day was just beginning.

■　■　■

"HEW is not studying the regulations, anymore," said a woman who worked in Congress and who had sneaked in the day before. She'd brought news.

"Califano is working on a major redirection," she said. "They have a list of issues. They're looking at potentially excluding a whole bunch of buildings and creating some sort of university consortium that allows colleges to avoid becoming accessible. It would essentially require disabled students to attend classes at only certain universities."

The news hit us like a ball full of lead.

Finally, Pat spoke. "It is still separate but equal in a new form."

"They're not taking us seriously at all." Kitty said what we were all thinking.

Not long after that, we got news that Denver and New York City had folded. The protesters had had no personal assistance or accessible bathrooms.

It was down to us and Los Angeles.

Sitting in Maldonado's office, looking at the somber faces around me, I felt like we were on the edge of a deep dark pit.

All of a sudden, a member of the outreach committee burst in.

"The governor of California wrote a letter to President Carter urging him to sign the regulations! We're getting help from all kinds of civil rights groups! The United Farm Workers sent a telegram of support signed by Cesar Chavez himself!"

We stared at her, unable to process what she was saying.

The governor of California? *And* Cesar Chavez, as in the famous civil rights leader for farmworkers? *That* Cesar Chavez?

We lifted our arms and cheered.

People were paying attention. They were listening. They supported us.

We just had to hold on and figure out how to turn up the volume on Califano.

We decided to go over Califano's head. We would try to get to President Carter.

■ ■ ■

The protesters filed into the conference room. People were starting to look a little unwashed and ragged. Everything depended on our ability to convince them to stay. We waited until every single person had arrived and the sign language interpreters were ready to start translating.

When it was quiet, I began to speak.

"The situation is this. President Carter knows where we stand. The White House is supposed to be calling us. The call has not come through yet.

"The shutdown is serious, but we are gaining momentum. In the last few hours, we've been getting national attention. An endorsement from Governor Brown has just come in.

"We cannot leave. LA is the only other sit-in still going, and they're holding on with just thirty-five people. We're the biggest.

"We are asking if you can you stay. Can you? Every day will make a difference."

I looked out at the crowd and held my breath. Please stay, I thought.

One by one, people raised their hands. They offered help.

"I can call the Black Panthers," said Brad Lomax, a young protester with multiple sclerosis. Brad used a wheelchair and favored suits with wide lapels. He was a member of the Black Panthers, who were Black revolutionaries famous for organizing in the Black community and protecting people from police brutality.

One hundred twenty-five protesters committed to staying.

I felt like we were in an enormous hot-air balloon that had almost crashed and then, out of nowhere, had been lifted by a massive gust of wind.

I started breathing again. Inadvertently, my brain shifted to the next problem.

How were we going to feed everyone?

■ ■ ■

We reconvened in Maldonado's office. I had to stop and get some water. I hadn't eaten for days. I was running on adrenaline.

"The shutdown is serious," I said.

Then Kitty asked something I hadn't thought about yet. "How are we going to stay in touch with our allies and the press?"

It was a good question. If we weren't in the news, we'd become irrelevant. Califano would win.

Then, someone, I don't remember who, had a brilliant idea: sign language.

We gave our announcements and messages to the deaf protesters. They took them to the windows looking out on the plaza where our supporters were holding a vigil. Once they got the attention of the deaf protesters and sign language interpreters outside, they signed our messages through the window. The deaf protesters and sign language interpreters then relayed the messages to the right people.

It was the perfect secret weapon.

■ ■ ■

Later that afternoon, we were in Maldonado's office trying to figure out food for our extremely large group, when one protester came rolling in fast.

"The Black Panthers are forcing their way into the building!"

Zooming out of the office, we rolled down the hallway just as the fourth-floor elevator doors slid open. Six tall men walked off the elevator carrying tubs.

"We've got dinner and snacks here," one of them told us. He was wearing a black leather jacket and a slouchy hat. "We told the security guards we'd stop at nothing to bring the media's attention on HEW if they didn't let us in and you guys got starved out." The Black Panthers had pushed their way into the building with fried chicken and vegetables, walnuts and almonds—food for all 125 of us. We gathered around and clapped.

The Black Panthers would bring us food every night for the rest of the protest.

That night, the news came out.

"They're tired. They're grubby. They're uncomfortable. But their spirits are soaring. The sit-in in the San Francisco HEW headquarters is now in its third day. A hundred and twenty-five disabled and handicapped are pledging they'll continue the sit-in through tomorrow night, if not longer. The squeeze is on, though. Hot water has been turned off on the fourth floor, where the occupation army of cripples has taken over."

CHAPTER THIRTEEN

THE GOVERNMENT THREATENS US WITH BOMBS

"Judy! Kitty! There's a bomb!"

A monitor rushed into Maldonado's office.

"Okay, what??" Kitty said.

I put my tea down. There goes my three minutes of shut-eye, I thought.

"The security guards say that we have to get everyone out of the building because there's a bomb."

Kitty and I looked at the monitor.

"Hmmm," Kitty said.

"What did they say *exactly*?" I asked.

"There were like three or four of those security guards that wear the big black boots. They came and found me and said, 'You have to get everyone out of the building, there's a bomb.' They had bomb-sniffing German shepherds with them."

Kitty and I looked at each other. She gave a little shrug. I knew what she was thinking. It was just way too coincidental.

"Well," I said, "I don't care. I'm going to bed. Tell them to wake me up when it goes off."

"Yup, me too," Kitty added.

We had to tell the protesters about the warning, just in case anybody wanted to leave. We called an emergency meeting and told them what the security guards had said. Nobody left.

■ ■ ■

The next morning, I woke up and looked at my watch. Five in the morning. The building was still standing.

It was Saturday, April 9, our fourth day in the building.

I poked Jim. "Let's get up. I want to wash my hair." I hate dirty hair.

Dressed and with nice clean hair, I sat talking with Jim for a minute while people slowly woke up around us. Jim drank a cup of coffee and I had some water. At that moment, another monitor found us.

"Judy, the last two pay phones are jammed. No one can make any calls."

We were totally cut off from making any outgoing calls.

■ ■ ■

That afternoon, President Carter's office called us.

"The president is aware of the situation in Los Angeles and San Francisco," a woman from the White House said. "He gives you his assurance that he will become personally involved in the issue of 504 and the issue of the regulations."

"Ha!" Kitty laughed. "He actually thinks we're going to buy that?"

We wrote a response and gave it to our signers at the window to communicate.

"We are encouraged by the contact made with the White House. However, the statement is not adequate, for Carter failed to address the primary reason for this sit-in. That is, the regulations of January 21 must be signed. The proposed changes from Califano are nonnegotiable. Califano is reviewing changes that are unacceptable and nonnegotiable."

The LA protesters got the same message from Carter's office and weren't sure what to do. They decided to leave the building.

We were the last city standing.

■   ■   ■

The next morning, I lay in bed and thought. Today was both Easter and the last day of Passover. Gazing at the ceiling, I decided I had to break my hunger strike. I needed all my strength and energy to think and strategize.

The security guards seemed to be feeling the holiday. They looked the other way when a bunch of protesters had their children brought into the building. The recreation committee had organized an egg hunt for the kids. Our supporters outside were still doing a nonstop protest.

So while the kids looked for Easter eggs and protesters rallied outside in full force, we sat in Maldonado's office talking on the telephone to Peter Libossi, the head lawyer of the Department of Health, Education, and Welfare. Peter had taken to calling us to check in every day—mainly, I think, to try to figure out if there was a way to get us to vacate the building. Talking with him was like a game of chicken. His goal was to try to persuade us to trust HEW and their process so we would leave, and our goal was to ferret as much information out of him as possible. He had to share some information with us to try to appear as if he was on our side—but not too much information and nothing that would harden our determination to stay.

Kitty and I and some of the others were sitting and listening to him talk when George Miller, a congressman from California, suddenly walked in unannounced. He picked up right away that we were on the phone with someone in DC and quietly walked over to another telephone to listen. That day Peter was sharing just a little too much and mentioned something about the changes that were being made to the regulations.

"Peter," he interrupted, "this is Congressman George Miller."

Peter stopped talking and hung up.

Congressman Miller put the phone down. He turned to look at all of us in the room. His face was dark.

"Stay," he said. "Stay in this building and don't leave until you've won."

■ ■ ■

By the end of Easter, we'd been in the building almost a week. We'd developed a kind of routine. There weren't many personal attendants left so the few who were still there were helping a lot of us. One of them would get Kitty up and give her a cup of coffee and then come see me to see what I needed. Everyone was getting dressed and doing whatever they needed to do in front of everybody. There was no privacy.

During the morning, the various committees would meet. The food committee planned meals, and the medications committee compiled a list of medication needs. In addition to the hot meals from the Black Panthers, all kinds of restaurants and churches were donating food. Local pharmacists were helping with medications and necessities.

One day after committee meetings were over, I was in Maldonado's office with Kitty and some of the others when we heard a crash from within the building. We rushed out and were just in time to see two protesters racing their wheelchairs down the hallway. Behind them were two more at the starting line. It looked like a relay. I laughed.

When I looked down the other end of the hallway, I saw a large group of people sitting in a circle on the floor singing while a guy played guitar. It feels like camp, I thought. And smiled.

In the afternoons, we'd hold a building-wide meeting of all the protesters. We'd share everything we knew about what was happening outside the building. We refused to begin the meetings until every single protester had arrived and the sign language interpreters were ready to start. We also insisted that the meetings not end until every last protester had had the chance to speak. One of the protesters could speak only by pointing to one letter at a time on his board, using a makeshift pointer stick attached to his head. But no matter how long it took for someone to talk, every single one of the now 150 protesters listened. Sometimes we were up until three in the morning.

The thing was, we didn't have to feel sorry for being slow or different in the building. Or for being a burden. We could make our own world, where the rules outside didn't apply. That outside world, which made us feel so isolated and wrong sometimes, felt very far away.

Hanging out

■ ■ ■

Some reporters were becoming captivated by us. A San
Francisco ABC News reporter borrowed a wheelchair
and used it all day in downtown San Francisco. Then
he reported on what it was like to live in America in
our shoes. Or socks, since I hardly ever wore shoes, to
tell the truth. I mean, why wear uncomfortable shoes
when you don't have to?

Protests all over the country were held in our honor.
We were becoming a part of something bigger than
ourselves.

CHAPTER FOURTEEN

WE THREATEN THE GOVERNMENT WITH MORE SLEEPOVERS

The following Friday, almost two weeks into the sit-in, Congressman Miller walked into the building with another congressman, Phillip Burton—and they declared room 406 to be a satellite office of Congress. They had decided to hold a congressional hearing, which is basically a type of meeting that congresspeople have when they want to call people's attention to something important. Congress can only make laws and oversee laws, which meant that it couldn't force the Department of Health, Education, and Welfare to sign the regulations—but it could hold a meeting and get a whole bunch of people to talk about the importance of Section 504. Which was a way to bring attention to our protest and pressure HEW into signing.

That day, room 406 was chock-full. There were people in wheelchairs, mentally disabled people, parents of disabled kids, deaf people signing, blind people with white canes and dogs, and all kinds of other disabled people, along with a sprinkling of reporters and media. To top it off, there were about eight hundred protesters gathered outside our building for a rally.

Congressman Burton opened the congressional hearing by stating that the intention of the meeting was to understand the nature of the conflict between us and HEW. A sign language interpreter stood next to him, translating in sign language. I spoke first.

"You have given us respectability," I said and thanked the congressmen. "We will not compromise any further. We will not be leaving this building until the regulations are signed as we want. This is a civil rights movement." I paused and then continued. "You are helping us start a civil rights movement."

Califano hadn't come to the hearing. Instead, he'd sent Gene Eidenberg, a kind of lower-level guy from the department.

Eidenberg read a statement from Califano, which essentially repeated what we already knew—that the regulations were under review.

"What is the delay with the regulations?" one of the congressmen asked Eidenberg. Eidenberg talked about some issue of studies and reviews, which made no sense.

"What studies are being done? And for what purpose exactly?"

Eidenberg flushed red. He tried to explain HEW's position but spoke so generally that nobody really understood what he was saying. He rambled. He dropped the news that the number of issues under review had reached a total of twenty-six.

And then, he mentioned the words "separate but equal."

Something exploded inside me.

No! I thought. No way could they still be thinking "separate but equal"! Would the idea of a "separate-but-equal" university ever be tolerated for any other group of people?

My insides burned.

Meanwhile, Kitty had turned her chair around, rolled out the door, and driven to the front of the building. Sitting in front of the enormous crowd outside, she told everyone what Eidenberg had said about a potential separate-but-equal university system.

The eight hundred protesters erupted in an uproar so loud it echoed inside the building.

■ ■ ■

It was my turn to give a reaction to the statement Eidenberg had read.

I didn't look at my notes.

Taking a deep breath, I looked directly at Eidenberg.

"Whether there was a Section 504," I said, my voice breaking, "there was a *Brown v. Board of Education*." My voice broke again. I looked down, swallowed hard, and looked back up at Eidenberg.

"The . . ." I stopped, suddenly overwhelmed by the weight and exhaustion of the days, weeks, and years of pushing. Of having to fight, just for an equal chance to live.

I took a deep breath and continued. "The harassment. The lack of equity that has been provided for disabled individuals, and that even now is being discussed by the administration, is so intolerable that I can't quite put it into words." I could not keep my voice from trembling. With every word, I felt a memory weighing. In my living room by myself, staring out the window, all my friends in school. At Brooklyn College weeping, as my father carried me onto the stage. Knocking on doors in my dorm, looking for help to go to the bathroom.

"I *can* tell you," I said, a force rising in me, "that every time you raise issues of separate but equal, the outrage of disabled individuals across this country is going to continue, is going to be ignited. And there will be more takeovers of buildings until finally, *maybe*, you'll begin to understand our position. We will no longer allow the government to oppress disabled individuals. We want the law enforced! We want no more segregation! We will accept no more discussions of segregation and . . ." I paused.

Eidenberg nodded sympathetically at me. The look on his face was unbearable.

"And, I would appreciate it if you would stop nodding your head in agreement when I don't think you have any idea what we are talking about!" I put my head in my hands, my body shaking.

■ ■ ■

The next hour of testimony was a blur. So many people spoke.

"What Califano forgets is that while they sit around and intellectualize, what they don't seem to understand is that our lives are not changed," said a woman from the Disability Rights Center.

"For one of the largest minorities in the country," Ed Roberts said, "I have never seen a better blueprint for segregation."

A woman who was developmentally disabled said, "I might seem second class to them, but I'm a person like everyone else. I don't think it's fair to be put down. I went to a special school for the mentally retarded. I didn't learn the things I should have. The attitude was I couldn't learn anyway, so why bother? I need help with some things, but not all."

In the midst of it all, Eidenberg flip-flopped. One minute he looked pitying and the next, furious.

Speaker after speaker got up—blind, deaf, physically disabled, former addicts, parents of disabled—all sharing their thoughts and feelings of pain, isolation, anger, and heartbreak; telling of years spent trying to get a job or an education, trying to count, trying to matter.

Suddenly, Eidenberg stood up from the table. Then he turned and ran out the door.

I looked at the congressmen. Everyone looked around at each other. What just happened? Did Eidenberg really just run out of the room?

Down the hallway, a door slammed.

Congressman Burton jumped up, red in the face. Then he turned around and dashed out the door after Eidenberg.

"Get out of there! Come out of there right now! Get out of there!" he yelled. Then we heard the sound of a door being kicked.

Utter silence.

"Come out here! Get out here right now!" Congressman Burton was livid.

Finally, we heard a door open.

Eidenberg walked back into the room, shadowed by Congressman Burton. He looked down, avoiding our eyes.

Fists clenched, Congressman Burton walked behind him, escorting him back to his chair. He stood behind Eidenberg and waited for him to sit down. Then he forced him to look at us.

The hearing continued. It was, in total, five hours of testimony.

Congressman Burton wrapped up the meeting. "I don't believe there is a person in this room who is not standing ten feet taller because of today," he said, his eyes wet.

■ ■ ■

After the hearing, we were sure we would hear something from Califano.

Nothing.

We met in Maldonado's office.

"How do we make it impossible for Califano to ignore us?" someone said.

"We have to raise the stakes," someone else said.

"What if we went directly to Califano?" I asked.

CHAPTER FIFTEEN

HOUSE PARTY AT CALIFANO'S

It turned out, not surprisingly, that Mr. Califano's house in Washington, DC, was located in a rather well-to-do neighborhood.

It was midnight and we were sitting in a circle in front of his house, singing and holding candles.

■ ■ ■

We'd arrived in Washington only four hours earlier, sweaty and dirty. After the congressional hearing, we'd asked all the protesters to vote on whether we should send a delegation to DC. It was unanimous, so the delegation had left San Francisco three days later.

We were met at the airport in Washington by a new supporter named Willy Dicks. The day after the congressional hearing, Willy had shown up at our building out of the blue, wanting to know how he could help us. Willy was a member of the Machinists Union, a labor union that supported machine workers. When we told him we needed money to fly thirty-four people to Washington, DC, he'd raised all of it *and* organized a place for us to stay.

The leaders of the Washington protesters, Frank Bowe and Eunice Fiorito, had also met us at the airport. Frank, who was deaf, had the wavy brown hair of a prep school boy. Eunice was tall and looked like a statue. She was blind and a good friend of mine. The minute they saw us, they'd immediately started apologizing for leaving the HEW offices in DC.

"We were starved out," Eunice had said.

"Eunice," I told her, "what happened to you was what motivated us to stay. We were totally outraged at how you were treated."

It was their apologies that had instigated our midnight visit to Mr. Califano's suburban neighborhood. The fact that Eunice and Frank felt like they'd done something wrong made me feel like a bull in front of a red flag. They weren't at fault. It was Califano, and we were not going to let him hide from us.

■ ■ ■

Willy and one of his friends from the Machinists Union had gotten a truck to haul us around in while we were in Washington. Once we'd managed to get all thirty-four of us out of the airport, Willy and his friend had loaded us into the back. It was about eleven at night, and the back of the truck was pitch-black. There were no windows, and no tie-downs or anything either. Which meant that when Willy drove down the street and turned the first corner, our wheelchairs slid clear across the bed of the truck.

"Whoa!" I shouted, grabbing air. We went around another corner and I lurched in the other direction. As we slid around the second time, something in me broke. I started giggling and couldn't stop. Then Kitty started giggling, and suddenly all of us were totally cracking up and crashing into each other.

■ ■ ■

When we finally got to Califano's house, the street was completely empty. One by one, the Machinists had unloaded us in the dark. We'd made a circle in front of the house and lit candles. We stayed there all night, singing.

Around six in the morning, the sun came up.

But there was no sign of Califano.

When it became clear that we weren't going to see Califano that morning, we piled back into the truck.

Well, Mr. Califano, I thought as we lurched around a corner, we'll be back.

The Machinists had arranged for us to stay in a church. They'd torn down walls in the bathroom and put in ramps to make the space accessible.

Next we needed breakfast and a plan. I felt like a car in fifth gear. We'd had no sleep for days, but I couldn't stop moving.

We gathered around a table in the back of the church to discuss tactics.

We knew we had to get Califano to quit ignoring us, but how? We decided it came down to three things that we had to accomplish.

Thing number one: Congress. We needed two big-wig senators to *publicly* state they were in agreement with the 504 regulations. *And* that they did not agree with any of the changes Califano was proposing. This would be a big deal. First of all, saying anything in public is a big deal to any senator. But for a senator to come out and say that they don't agree with the way a federal department is handling something is an even bigger deal.

Thing number two: President Carter. We had to reach as high as we could, which meant the White House. If not President Carter himself, then we needed one of his top people to say that they supported us and 504. *Publicly.*

Also a pretty major deal.

Thing number three: discomfort. We needed Mr. Califano to feel *really* uncomfortable. Which meant more candlelight visits to his nice suburban house and more demonstrations. Ideally with lots of press coverage.

Then, strategy session over, we'd gotten on the phone. Within minutes, we'd organized two key meetings.

We packed ourselves into the truck and drove to Capitol Hill.

■ ■ ■

Senator Alan Cranston was tall and bald with a sharp-looking nose. He was also a very powerful politician.

That meant that Senator Cranston, a Democrat from California, was our number one congressional target. Getting him to publicly state that he supported us could be the first domino to fall.

We piled into his office.

Okay, I thought, how is this going to go? A bubble formed in my stomach.

The senator started the meeting by telling us that he thought what we'd done by taking over the federal building was "reasonable."

Which right away made me say a little internal, "Phew!" because, in political-speak, the word "reasonable" holds some serious weight. Basically, in this context, "reasonable" can be loosely translated as: "okay, you did something really big. In fact, some people might see what you did as outrageous, but I'm cool with it."

The senator continued. "I do think the people responsible for the laws should hear from the people affected."

Which, in political-speak, basically meant: "Okay, I agree. It's ridiculous you haven't been consulted."

One hurdle down.

At that point, the senator got to the meat of the question at hand.

"I'm not an administration spokesman," he said.

Uh-oh, I thought, trouble. Because what he was really saying was, "Sorry guys, I'm not sticking my neck out for you."

I rubbed my sweaty palms on my legs.

"We've sought meetings with President Carter and Secretary Califano. We were unsuccessful," I told him.

"You are prejudging their changes. The Carter administrative changes may make the regulations more effective."

My stomach wrenched.

How could he say that? How could he say that we should be consulted and then—literally one second later—say the administration might know more about what we needed than we did ourselves? This was the *exact* problem.

The senator had a list of the changes proposed by the department. Although the list seemed to increase daily, it boiled down to ten main points. Every single one of them watered down the regulations.

Cranston wanted to go through the issues, one by one. I wanted to scream. *How can you possibly be debating with us about what we think is best for our own lives?*

But I forced myself to breathe and respond.

One by one, we explained why the changes weren't okay with us.

When we were done, Cranston leaned back in his chair and crossed his legs. This man had so much power over our fate, I thought. We were completely dependent on his opinion of us. It was so unfair.

"I still don't see why I should support you publicly," he said. Next to him, I saw the glow disappear from Kitty's face. She looked ashen.

I cleared my heart from my throat.

"Senator Cranston," I said. "Congress has the power to bring the executive branch up before you. You've got to take more than a passive position."

The room felt like the mouth of a volcano. The senator looked at me.

Then one of our people brought up the idea that Califano had proposed: to make universities separate but equal. It was the one item we hadn't discussed yet.

The senator frowned.

"Separate but equal is not acceptable," he said. He drew his words out slowly, while we hung on every single one. "I cannot believe that there is any deliberate desire to continue discrimination." His mouth tightened. I held my breath.

"But," he continued, "I agree. Costs should not be an issue here. I will make a statement. A consortium is not acceptable. That will be in my statement."

He would support us. Publicly.

I exhaled. Suddenly, out of nowhere, I was flooded with a wave of exhaustion.

Then Frank Bowe stood up. He looked exhausted too. But Frank's eyes were alive with something deep and dark. He looked directly at Senator Cranston and spoke, our sign language interpreter translating.

"Senator," he signed, "we're not even second-class citizens." He paused, his face unbelievably weary. "We're third-class citizens."

At that moment, something heavy entered our bodies. It weighed on us, pulling us down into our seats. We knew Frank was right. We were third-class citizens.

The enormous bubble that had been growing in my chest through the whole meeting suddenly popped. Tears washed through my entire body.

But there was no time to stop. We had to keep going. We rolled next to Senator Harrison Williams's office.

The senator met with us and didn't sit down. He stood attentively and listened, his dark bushy eyebrows serious.

I was direct.

"This is a request for another statement from you in cooperation with Senator Cranston." We updated him on the regulations and told him that Senator Cranston had said he would issue a statement.

Senator Williams agreed to team up with Cranston on the statement. The meeting went very fast. A couple of us fell asleep halfway through.

Thing number one: check.

CHAPTER SIXTEEN

THERE ARE NO ACCESSIBLE BATHROOMS IN THE WHITE HOUSE

W e went back to the church to regroup.
After the meeting with Senator Cranston on Capitol Hill, I got the feeling that some of our people were starting to believe we might win, but I was not one of them yet. Okay, I thought, we're making progress. But, I also thought, things aren't done until they're done. Like written in stone, kind of done.

We spent the rest of the day working on getting a meeting with the White House. We called staffers, congressional representatives, friends. Basically we called anyone with power who would talk to us. Finally, we got a meeting for the next day. It was with one of the president's head honchos, Stuart Eizenstat, domestic policy adviser. He was in charge of any policy that dealt with what happened inside America—as opposed to foreign policy, which is what happens with other countries.

We prepared for the meeting for a long time. I actually don't know what time it was when we went to bed, but I do know it was well past midnight.

I'll be honest, little mattresses on hard wooden church floors aren't super comfortable to sleep on, but I fell asleep the second my head hit the, uh, "bed."

The next morning, we woke up, had breakfast, and drove to the White House.

■　■　■

They blocked us at reception. Several guards stood in front of the doors.

"You are not allowed to enter," the receptionist told us, looking dead serious. "Unless you swear that you will not start a sit-in in the White House."

Wait, what, *really*? I thought. They're afraid of us?

I couldn't stop a smile from curling across my face.

■　■　■

Stuart Eizenstat seemed pretty young. He also had neatly combed hair and glasses.

I started the meeting. I told him how we felt about how Califano had treated the DC protesters. Then I briefed him on the history of the regulations, just to be sure he knew what we were talking about, and told him how much the regulations were now being weakened. Eizenstat kept quiet while I spoke and then he responded.

"We in the domestic policy staff coordinate to make sure the legislation we propose is consistent with the president's policy," he said. "We have not gotten involved with regulations before."

What he meant was, "Not our job, guys. Sure, we represent the president to make sure all the proposed laws are in line with what he said he'd do, but that doesn't include regulations."

Here we go again, I thought.

"Section 504 is a major social change," one of the protesters pointed out.

"No other civil rights laws have had costs implied," I said. This was a big thing people just didn't get. One of the main objections companies had to 504 was that it would cost money to put in ramps or elevators or make any of the other needed changes. But our argument was: So what? No civil rights laws had any footnotes, like "by the way, we will only do the work we need to do to ensure people have equal access to stuff when it doesn't cost me any money."

Eizenstat was taking notes.

"With respect," I said. My voice cut like a knife. "We have the support of labor and other organizations of minority groups. The disability organizations are strong, and yet we feel we are being led around. Few other sets of regulations have had to go through the ordeal we have been led through. Nondisabled individuals are telling us they know best."

Then Eizenstat put down his notebook. He looked at us.

"I believe it is time for the administration to take a position," he said quietly.

I let out my breath. I hadn't even realized I'd been holding it.

The White House would support us. Publicly.

Thing number two: check.

■ ■ ■

Rolling out of Eizenstat's office, we asked a man where we could find an accessible bathroom. He didn't know. He actually had to ask someone to go find one for us. Then he came back and told us we had to *leave* the White House, cross the street, and go to an entirely different building. Either there were no people who used wheelchairs in the White House, or those poor people were running across the street every single time they had to go to the bathroom. I'm guessing it was the former.

■ ■ ■

We drove back to our church. Some people went to dinner. I got on the phone. I wanted to call the protesters in San Francisco to make sure we were holding strong in the federal building. They were eager to know what was happening in Washington. I updated them on everything and we hung up.

■ ■ ■

At about ten that night, our group in Washington convened to decide next steps.

Right away it emerged that most of our people wanted to go back to San Francisco.

"With Senator Cranston and the White House both supporting us, Califano is definitely going to sign the regulations," said one protester. My heart sank. I really didn't want to argue. Fighting among ourselves was a sure way to fail. But I totally disagreed.

"The regulations haven't actually been signed yet. And 'almost there' is not 'there.'"

A group of protesters shook their heads.

"But they will sign," one said. "We can't risk looking like we're unwilling to compromise," said another.

My stomach wrenched. A fleeting vision passed in front of my eyes: me, thanking person after person for helping me up a step into the bathroom. I was so tired of being grateful for being able to go to the bathroom. What haven't we compromised? I thought.

"We have compromised our whole lives," I said, trying to keep the edge out of my voice. "And we're so close now to winning."

"Judy," someone said. "We're filthy, we're sweaty, and we're wrung out. We want to go home."

■ ■ ■

Finally, after hours of arguing, we agreed to let the San Francisco protesters decide what we should do. We got our lead people on the phone in San Francisco and explained the situation. Can you put the question to the protesters? Should we stop or should we keep going? Ask them to vote, we said.

Thirty minutes later, they called us back.

The protesters had voted to stay the course. We would continue.

It was five in the morning when we went to bed.

CHAPTER SEVENTEEN

PLEASE DON'T IGNORE US OR WE WILL COME TO YOUR SUNDAY SCHOOL

I couldn't sleep.

I lay awake looking at the ceiling, reviewing every decision we'd ever made in my head.

Before he was elected, Carter had promised he would sign the regulations. Based on that promise, we'd worked for him and supported his campaign.

But here he was, choosing money and convenience over us. Over our civil rights. Over our lives.

Our protest was teetering on the edge. People were running dry. How long did we have before everything fell apart?

A ball of fire formed in my stomach.

I saw our sign language interpreter pass by me and decided to get up.

"Pssst, can you help me get into my chair?" I whispered. Most people were still sleeping, but as she helped me go to the bathroom a few others also got up.

I sat in my chair. It was getting warm in DC. I wiped my forehead. I smelled terrible and my hair was greasy.

I just couldn't believe Califano was still ignoring us. What did we have to do?

■ ■ ■

I looked around the church. And then I said to everyone who was awake:

"Let's go meet with Califano."

Ten of us loaded into the truck and drove to the Department of Health, Education, and Welfare.

The front of the building was glass doors, which were blocked by about six tough-looking guards wearing black boots and holding clubs.

We rolled up to the doors. I was about to enter when a guard intercepted me.

"Sorry, ma'am," he said. "You can't enter here."

"I'm here to meet with Secretary Califano," I told him, calmly. He must be confused, I thought. There's no way they can block everyday citizens from entering a government building.

"Sorry, ma'am," the guard repeated. "I can't let you in."

The fire in my stomach burned.

"I'm a citizen," I told him. "I have the right to meet with Secretary Califano. Can I speak with your manager?"

"Sorry, ma'am," he repeated in the exact same tone, for the third time. "I can't let you do that."

All of a sudden it dawned on me.

They were refusing to allow *me* in. Not everyone. Me.

Us.

They must be under specific orders to watch out for people in wheelchairs trying to get into the building.

I felt like I'd been slapped across the face.

My jaw clenched.

How many times had I been blocked from going somewhere? Told I couldn't get in? Told, "No, not you"?

Buses, planes, schools, restaurants, theaters, offices, friends' houses flashed through my mind.

I was sick of being blocked.

I didn't care if it was a guard, a bus driver, a pilot, a principal, a manager, or a step. It was all the same. They were all the same.

The ball of fire inside me erupted.

I turned my chair around and backed up.

Sitting a small distance away, I looked at the guard.

I flicked a switch and drove my chair directly toward the building, toward the guards at full speed.

Maybe they thought I'd stop. They were wrong. At the last minute, they jumped aside.

I smashed into the door.

The other protesters followed me in their chairs.

Frozen, the guards watched us.

Over and over again we turned around. Slamming into the doors.

SMASH, SMASH, SMASH.

Suddenly, the guards came alive, like a spell had been lifted. Armed and in uniform, they kicked our chairs.

■ ■ ■

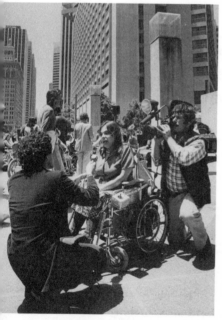
Me talking to the press

Later, when I was interviewed about the incident, I spoke the truth.

Secretary Califano is "arrogant, obstinate, and absolutely inhumane," I told a reporter. "The regulations are our lifeblood and he still refuses to even meet with us."

In response, Califano's spokesperson claimed our charges related to the 504 regulations were inaccurate.

That was Friday. The eighteenth day of the protest.

■ ■ ■

We decided to hold a massive rally in front of the
White House. Over the weekend, using the Machinists'
headquarters as home base, we prepped. We had to get
people mobilized, figure out transportation, plan the
agenda, invite speakers, and work the press. The organizing was a big deal, but it wasn't what worried me
the most. What worried me the most was the heat of
disapproval I could feel from the Washington, DC, protesters. They thought I was going too far. And maybe I
was. But the lesson I had learned at my family dinner
table was embedded in my blood.

If you believe in something, do whatever you have
to do to get your point across.

Speak loudly. Interrupt.

Get in their face.

■ ■ ■

On Saturday night, we left our prepping for the
rally to pay another nighttime visit to Califano's
house. But again, he avoided us and left through his
back door.

The next morning was Sunday. We decided to go
sit outside President Carter's church. While President
Carter was teaching Sunday school inside, we were
sitting outside with our "Sign 504" posters. Afterward

the president and his wife slipped out the back. The newspapers wrote about all of it.

Then it was Tuesday, the day of our rally in front of the White House. It was sunny and clear.

Dog-tired, we piled into the truck and drove to Lafayette Park in front of the White House. We got busy, assembling a stage and a sound system. While we were working, people began walking and rolling into the park from every direction.

We had a hundred protesters and a long list of high-powered speakers, including five congressmen. Bands played and we sang songs. The sign language interpreters translated on stage. People held signs like "How can we get on the bandwagon when we can't get on the bus?" Sitting in the park, next to Kitty, watching everyone come together while the sun set behind them, I felt a warmth spread through my chest.

That night we decided to send most of our people home to San Francisco. The protesters in the federal building needed reinforcements, and people just wanted to go home.

The next day, everyone but six of us left.

■ ■ ■

Those of us who were left behind wanted to pay Califano a visit, but we needed to know what he was up to. We did some reconnaissance. Without too much effort, we discovered he was scheduled to give a talk at the National Press Club for reporters. We got back in the truck and headed downtown.

■　■　■

When we got to the building, they wouldn't let us in.

Sitting outside, we regrouped. Because it was a press event, there was one person among us who they couldn't keep out. Remember the San Francisco reporter who had borrowed a wheelchair to try to get around San Francisco? He, Evan White, had flown to Washington with us to follow our story, and he was with us that day. What happened next, is what we heard afterward from Evan.

First, Evan used his press card to get into Califano's talk. Then, as one of the reporters in the room, he asked Califano questions about us and the sit-in.

Califano refused to answer him.

After the talk was over, Califano left the room. Evan and his cameraman followed him with a camera and a microphone, asking him more questions.

Califano ignored him and kept walking. He headed for an elevator.

When the elevator door opened, Califano stepped in. Evan tried to follow but Califano's guards blocked him from entering. The elevator door closed on Evan's face and he turned to leave.

But then the elevator car accidentally returned to where Evan was standing. The door slid open and revealed Califano facing the hallway. Pushing the microphone into Califano's face while his cameraman filmed, Evan asked Califano a series of questions.

"What is the status on the 504 regulations? Will you sign the regulations as they were drafted?"

Califano refused to respond. But the cameraman captured all of it.

Using the video of Califano stubbornly keeping his mouth closed, Evan reported on the incident in the news.

After that, everyone became certain that Califano was going to sign the regulations. Everyone, that is, except me.

It's probably very likely that Califano will sign now, I thought. But not signed is not signed. I just didn't trust that he wouldn't try to wriggle away again.

The next day, I stayed in Washington with Pat Wright while everyone else went back to the federal building in San Francisco.

CHAPTER EIGHTEEN

POWER TO THE PEOPLE

Pat and I were in a restaurant. In the corner, a television blared. We were talking about what to do next when, out of the corner of my eye, I noticed that the news had started.

"Today, at the Department of Health, Education, and Welfare . . . ," an announcer began.

That caught our attention. Pat and I looked up.

Now what? I thought. Butterflies took flight in my stomach.

"Joseph Califano," the announcer continued, "Secretary of Health, Education, and Welfare, has signed . . ."

Suddenly everything around me went blurry. Was the reporter speaking in slow motion? I thought. I couldn't understand. What was she saying?

". . . the enabling regulations for Section 504 of the Rehabilitation Act of 1973."

Goosebumps rose all over my body.

Pat and I looked at each other.

We looked back at the TV.

And then, we raised our arms and cheered.

■ ■ ■

It was Thursday, April 28, the twenty-fourth day of the sit-in. It had been almost a month since I'd packed my toothbrush and underwear in my backpack and headed to San Francisco.

The regulations had been signed. Unchanged.

Exactly what we wanted.

■ ■ ■

On the fourth floor of the San Francisco Federal Building, a party erupted. People danced, hugged, laughed, and cried. The music went all night.

The next day, nobody wanted to leave.

In the cocoon of the building, something had happened.

"We all feel in love with each other," one protester told a reporter.

"I've discovered that I count as a person," said another.

"Instead of seeing myself as a weak person, I found my strength reinforced by others like me," said someone else.

"I'm going to miss them," said a federal guard, who had started learning sign language. He hoped one day to become a sign language interpreter. "They were real nice people."

None of us expected to feel as heartbroken as we did.

They decided to spend one last night together in the building to celebrate.

■ ■ ■

On Saturday morning, April 30, twenty-six days after the first rally outside the building, over one hundred people left the federal building for the last time.

They hugged the guards goodbye.

Forming one long line onto the building's plaza, they emerged into the sunlight.

An enormous crowd waited for them, clapping.

Carrying backpacks and bags and flashing victory signs, the protesters smiled and waved. Together, they sang "We Have Overcome," their own version of the famous civil rights song "We Shall Overcome."

And the enormous crowd waved back and chanted, "Power to the people!"

PART THREE

FOUR YEARS LATER

CHAPTER NINETEEN

THIRTY-SIX
MILLION OF US

For those of us at the Center for Independent Living in Berkeley, the years following the signing of the 504 regulations were total chaos. The thing is, getting a law passed doesn't necessarily make it happen right away. Ramps and elevators and things had to actually be put into schools and buses before we could access them.

The other problem was that a lot of people didn't want to put in the work to integrate the schools, make the buildings accessible, or do any of the other things that the regulations required. Which meant we had to stay on top of them. The association in charge of the bus system, for example, sent out a letter that said it was going to cost too much money to make the bus system accessible.

Do you know what some of the laziest arguments against change are? It's too expensive, it's too unsafe, and it's just impossible. That's what people were saying.

So we did our homework and figured out that the bus association was wrong. Putting a wheelchair lift in a bus would cost just about the same as putting in air conditioning, which was totally doable for the bus system. Basically, when they'd estimated how many people would be taking the bus—and how much money they'd make from bus fares—they assumed that most disabled people wouldn't use the bus. That was a huge, erroneous presumption, so we corrected them.

The truth is, it's the easiest thing in the world to say no. Especially if you work in business or finance. But we were talking about civil rights and, like I've said, no other civil rights issue had ever been questioned about costs.

In the aftermath of 504, the challenge—or the opportunity, depending on how you look at it—was on us. We had to challenge the naysayers by working on solutions. When people made ridiculous statements saying this or that was impossible, we had to respond. We also had to help people see that when things were made accessible, everyone would benefit, not just disabled people.

■ ■ ■

For the first few years, I was in Berkeley working at the Center for Independent Living. We had become famous. People from all over the world had heard about our sit-in and wanted to know more about what we were doing and what had led to such massive protests. The British news and Japanese news teams came and interviewed us for television. This tickled me. I felt very connected to the world thanks to the international calls but also because my parents were from Germany, although we never talked about that.

A few years back, before the sit-in, I'd decided to visit Europe. My brother and I asked my parents for permission to go to Germany. My mother and father had very bad feelings about the country because the Nazis had murdered their parents in concentration camps, so we weren't sure how they would feel about us visiting. No one in my family had been to Germany since my parents had left as kids. But they agreed we should go.

My father connected us with an old friend from his village. The man picked us up and took us to see where my father had grown up. The people we met, none of whom were Jews, were very kind.

But the thing is, not one word was said about what had happened to the Jews. Even when they took us to my father's old house and showed us pictures of my father and his brothers. Even when they showed us the site where the synagogue had been burned down.

Have you ever noticed how people don't like to talk about things that make them uncomfortable?

Why didn't the principal let me into kindergarten?

Silence.
Why aren't we allowed on buses?
Silence.
Why can't disabled people teach?
Silence.
Where are all the Jews going?
Piercing silence.

■ ■ ■

I refuse to give in to silence.
This is one of the things about me, I think. I persist.
I insist on speaking. And being heard.

■ ■ ■

In Germany, I went to the Paralympics, which are Olympics for people with disabilities. I met disabled people from South America and Africa and all over the world. I saw how people from certain countries were much poorer than people from other countries. Even among the Paralympians, who are among the elite athletes of their countries, there was a huge difference.

After Germany, I went to Sweden on a program that allowed me to learn about Sweden's government and their "social welfare system," which basically is how

Sweden takes care of its people. This opened my eyes to the fact that how we do things in the United States is not the same as how other countries do things.

I became friends with other disabled activists, like Kalle Konkkola who was a young Finnish activist who'd had polio, and Adolf Ratzka, a young German activist who also had had polio. We were all unique for the times. We were disabled but we'd gone to college anyway. We'd challenged the system that dictated how we had to be taken care of and we'd turned it on its head. We weren't ashamed of who we were and what we needed, and we were no longer willing to allow charity organizations, focused on finding a "cure," speak for us. We started working together.

At heart, I am a networker and a convener, which basically means I meet people and introduce them to other people. I suck up as much information as I can and try to share it with as many people as I can.

■　■　■

Not too long after I got back from Europe, my fellow activists and I started talking about the fact that Section 504 didn't prohibit discrimination everywhere and we needed legislation that did.

■　■　■

In 1980, President Ronald Reagan created a government committee called the National Council on Disability. The purpose of this new committee was to advise the president on ideas for policies for people with disabilities. This committee was a big deal, and President Reagan appointed a guy named Justin Dart to the committee.

Justin Dart always wore a cowboy hat and cowboy boots. Like me, he'd had polio and used a wheelchair. He'd also started a company that was very successful. He was a Republican who came from a wealthy Republican family in Chicago. He was very respectful of everyone and so he was respected by everyone. Justin was zealous about civil rights for people with disabilities.

The first thing Justin did as one of the leaders of the National Council on Disability, was to figure out a way to meet with disability activists across America. He wanted to hear what they had to say about whatever problems they were facing and learn what a civil rights act for disabled people might look like. He decided to travel around the country. Everywhere he went, he met with local disability leaders and got their feedback on creating a national policy. This was a time when traveling with a wheelchair was not only hard and complicated but expensive. The government wouldn't pay for it. So Justin paid for it himself. That just shows you what kind of man Justin was.

When Justin got back from his trip, he got together with a couple of other people from the National Council on Disability. They wrote down all the ideas for what a civil rights act for disability should look like. Then they sent it to the rest of the committee members to see what they thought.

Well, a lot of people on the committee didn't like it.

It was as if Justin had proposed that the government buy monkeys and unicorns for all disabled people.

Civil rights for disabled people all over the place, everywhere? they said. That sounds radical. And *expensive.*

Who decided it was a good idea to ask disabled people what *they* wanted?

It was ridiculous, they said.

Ludicrous.

Nonsense.

Then the head of the National Council on Disability stood up. It was a man named Joseph Dusenbury. He waited for everyone to calm down. Finally, everyone stopped arguing and looked at him.

"Ladies and gentlemen," Joseph said, "this document was written by the disabled people of the United States. I want to hear a motion to approve this document, and I don't want you to change a single word."

The council was quiet. They took another vote.

And the document was approved.

．．．

This is when I got more involved. Because, at that point, disability activists from across the country began to talk about this proposed national policy on disability.

And as more and more disabled people and allies heard about it, a movement grew in support. Like a roar.

Simultaneously, however, a movement was mounted against us.

The movement against civil rights for disabled people came from many directions. Including from the president.

President Reagan—who was probably thinking something like, "Hey, National Council on Disability, I didn't think you'd do something *this* big!"—was also trying to weaken laws that had already been passed.

We had to fight to keep the laws in place and we had to fight for any disabled people who went to court. Like a hearing-impaired woman who was denied entrance to a nursing program. That court battle went all the way to the Supreme Court, which ruled that the woman's hearing impairment did actually disqualify her from participating in the nursing program.

When I heard this, my stomach dropped. This was a very negative interpretation of the meaning of Section 504. How would any judges in the future interpret Section 504?

Our legal organization battled back.

Then another case came to the Supreme Court. It was about a man who had lost his arm in an accident and then was denied a job at the company where he'd worked before the accident. It was a question of discrimination. Disability lawyers proved that this issue concerned not just this one man but millions of Americans.

The court ruled in our favor and confirmed that the employer was, indeed, discriminating against the man.

It was an enormous victory.

■ ■ ■

In the meantime, remember how it's Congress that makes the laws? Justin and the people at the National Council on Disability were gathering information that would be needed to convince Congress to propose and pass a law. If people with disabilities needed a civil rights act, that meant we had to show Congress that discrimination against disabled people was a huge problem. So Justin and the other council members wrote a long report and included the stories that Justin had heard across the country about all the problems disabled people faced. Then they sent it to Congress and President Reagan and recommended the passage of a comprehensive law requiring equal opportunity for people with disabilities.

A top guy at the White House called Justin.

"What were you folks thinking about with this civil rights thing?" the staff person said. "The president won't touch it with a ten-foot pole. Take it out."

Justin hung up and went to meet with the assistant attorney general of civil rights, Bradford Reynolds, who was basically the second head guy for civil rights in the country.

"Bradford," he said, "I do not believe that Ronald Reagan wants to go down in history as the president who opposed keeping the promise of the Declaration of Independence to thirty-five million Americans with disabilities."

Silence.

Not too long after, President Reagan agreed to support the proposal.

■ ■ ■

So, yup, we were busy. We had Justin and the council members standing up to the president of the United States. We had our disability lawyers battling in court. And we had the disability activists organizing protests and huge letter-writing campaigns. One of the things the protesters were doing then was stopping public transit buses, then propelling themselves out of their wheelchairs and dragging themselves up the bus steps.

■ ■ ■

In 1988, Congress decided to investigate the information presented by Justin and the National Council on Disability. Which basically means that Justin and the council had successfully convinced some of the congresspeople that a law might be needed. Their first step was to create a task force that would collect more information for Congress.

Justin hit the road again. Crisscrossing American yet again, he met thousands of people and wrote down what they told him about their experiences with disability discrimination. He shared it with the task force.

The next step? Congress had to convene one of their committees to listen to what people with disabilities had to say.

Seven hundred people went. Blind people, deaf people, parents of disabled people, and people with HIV infection. I went too.

At the end of that meeting, two senators—Edward Kennedy and Tom Harkin—finally made a public commitment to bringing a civil rights act to Congress. They called it the Americans with Disabilities Act.

Within two years, everything would have to be made accessible. Everything.

■　■　■

Remember my friend Pat from the sit-in? She became the general of the disability activist groups. She had thousands of soldiers across America, organizing protests and making sure everyone's story got told.

Thirty-six million of us were finally being given the chance to speak.

■ ■ ■

In 1989, the Senate passed the Americans with Disabilities Act.

But then it got stuck in the House of Representatives.

This made us mad.

■ ■ ■

The United States Capitol building, which is the office of Congress, is impressive. It's almost as tall as the Statue of Liberty and it looks like it's straight from ancient Greece. The Capitol symbolizes democracy, which is all about creating a government that allows people to have a voice in deciding what is best for them.

But Congress had stopped listening.

■ ■ ■

Our people came to the US Capitol from all over the country. To reach the main entrance to the building, you must climb eighty-three marble steps. The protesters assembled at the bottom of those steps.

It was an unusually hot day in early spring. Justin Dart spoke. "Two centuries is long enough for people with disabilities to wait before the constitutional promise of justice is kept."

Then, slowly, one by one, people pushed themselves out of their wheelchairs and fell onto the bottom step.

Some inched forward on their backs. Others slithered on their bellies, with their legs trailing behind.

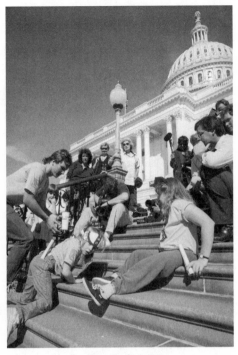
Crawling up the Capitol steps

Using elbows, knees, and shoulders to pull themselves up, they dragged themselves up to the second step.

One was Jennifer Keelan, an eight-year-old girl with cerebral palsy. A little while before, Jennifer had gone to a restaurant to eat with her family. But when they asked for a table, Jennifer was told to go away.

"No one wants to watch you eat," a waitress told her.

She'd come all the way from Arizona to join the protest on the Capitol steps.

■ ■ ■

Jennifer was lying flat on her belly, like a caterpillar.
Her elbows and knees dug into the step to drag her
body. Her lip was bloody from when she had fallen and
her face had hit the hard marble. She was sweaty and
wore a red, white, and blue bandana around her head.
Lying on the second step, she raised her head to look at
the step above her. Several volunteers stood around her,
ready to offer help.

"Water?" she asked.

Someone gave her a drink of water and then she
climbed the third step.

Eighty more to go.

It was March 12, 1990. Nine long years had passed
since Justin first toured the country. The protesters
wanted Congress to see the indignity that we were
forced to live with every single day in a country that refused to end the segregation of people with disabilities.

■ ■ ■

Hours later, Jennifer dragged herself up the seventy-
seventh step. Still, volunteers stood by, ready to help.
But she didn't want help.

"I'll do it," she said, "if it takes me all night."

■ ■ ■

Four months later, the US House of Representatives finally passed the Americans with Disabilities Act.

July 26, 1990, was glorious. Washington was hot and humid and covered in the glistening green of thousands of trees, while the deepest of blues were above. With three thousand people, I sat on the South Lawn of the White House. President George H. W. Bush walked across the lawn and stood in front of us. Justin Dart was at his side. A hush fell over the enormous crowd.

"Let the shameful wall of exclusion finally come tumbling down," said President Bush.

And he sat down at a desk and signed the Americans with Disabilities Act into law.

As I sat, twenty years flashed through my mind.

The yelling of the commuters, as we sat in the middle of Madison Avenue. The college girl's face, as she asked if I might know anyone who could join her on her date. My father's jaw clenched, as he carried me onto the stage to get my high school award. My mother, as she lay out my dress for the first day of kindergarten.

Maldonado's face as he looked at us, and it dawned on him that, just maybe, we weren't going to leave.

I was forty-one years old and I was finally an equal citizen.

AND NEXT

The plane landed with a bump. Two airline staff helped me transition from my seat into my wheelchair, and we rolled into the airport. I'd only been in my new role with the World Bank for a short time. My job was focused on pushing disability rights forward around the world.

The people who were supposed to meet us to take us to the hotel, arrived with a van. As they packed our things into the back, I looked out the window. This was my first trip to India.

We drove out to the road. Cars hurtled by at what seemed like a thousand miles an hour. It was like someone had flipped a switch and put the world in turbo speed. Busy people were everywhere. Some stood on the side of the highway and sold what looked like bags of juice. Others walked with briefcases, crossing rapidly between the cars, little clouds of dust rising with each step. In the shade of a truck, kids lay on their bellies and played a game with dice. In the other direction, a circle of grandmas sat on a blanket and talked.

Where were my people, I wondered?

Then I saw them.

First, I saw a man. He crawled on the side of the road, his legs small and thin. They dragged behind him, as he pulled himself forward. The upper part of his body looked strong and powerful and he moved fast, kicking up dirt and debris from the road. His face and body were almost entirely covered in dust. In his right hand, he gripped a small metal bowl. As I watched, he pulled himself into a seated position next to a stopped car, his legs tucked underneath him. He held his bowl out to the car window. A hand from inside the car reached out and dropped a coin into the metal bowl. The man took it, put the bowl in his mouth to carry it, and dragged himself back to the side of the road.

A few feet away was a woman, sitting on a small piece of cardboard. Each time a car whizzed by, a cloud of litter from the road—empty plastic bottles, little pieces of cartons, plastic wrappings—rose toward her face. Each time, she held a small metal bowl out toward the cars and said something.

People call them "the crawlers," said my colleague next to me in the van.

My stomach twisted.

These were the disabled people. Not all of them, but the disabled people without jobs and wheelchairs or protection from the government. They were forced to crawl through the streets and beg for food. I guessed that the man with the thinner legs had had polio.

"That would be me," I thought, "if I'd been born in India."

We turned off the main road and drove onto a side street. Sitting on the corner were more crawlers. But these were small children, some blind, others with an injured limb, some missing an arm or leg. They looked too young to be out on their own. They were somewhere between five and seven years old. Some were holding little bowls out to the masses of men and women walking by; others poked through a pile of garbage. As I watched, one of them picked something out of the pile, examined it, and popped it in his mouth. Most of the people walking by completely ignored them and passed by without a second glance. I craned my head to watch them as we sped by, hoping I'd see someone stop to pay attention, give them money, do something.

"Most of them weren't born with disabilities," my colleague said, as I watched. "They come from poor families who have no choice but to sell them to gangs. The gangs injure them to make them look pathetic and then force them to beg for money, which they take."

Tears rose in my eyes. I wanted to do something, anything, take them all home with me.

But I knew I couldn't save them that way, that it didn't work like that. And even if I could, I would only save those eight, but there were thousands more. All over the world.

No, my job was to get the world to stop ignoring them. To stop pretending like they didn't exist. To actually see them. And then, to let them be just like everyone else, so they could go to school, get jobs, have wheelchairs, have a life.

■ ■ ■

A few days after my arrival, we drove to a remote village in India.

The air felt like a hot washcloth pressed against my face. Beads of sweat dripped down my forehead, but I barely noticed. All I saw were the people circled around me.

"It was this boy," one of the men said, leaning on a pair of crutches, one leg visibly smaller than the other. Lifting one of his crutches, he gestured to a little boy sitting at his mother's feet. The boy appeared to be about two years old. He had brown curly hair. Feeling our gaze on him, he looked up at us and an enormous grin spread across his face. I couldn't help but grin back, his smile was so infectious.

The man on crutches continued. "His mother came to us when he was just a few days old and asked for our help. 'My mother-in-law has told me not to feed my child,' she told us. 'Because he was born without arms, she wants me to let him die.'" The man stopped. I looked at the circle of faces looking at me.

My heart felt like lead.

"We went to the police," a woman in a wheelchair picked up the story. "And told them what the grandmother had said. They came and talked to her and forced her to stop pressuring the mother. And now, you see, the boy is strong."

I looked down at the boy. Between the first two toes on his right foot, he gripped a marker and drew on a piece of paper that someone had given him as we were talking.

■　■　■

This circle of disabled people had become disability rights activists. They were telling me about how much pressure there was on people who had children with disabilities, pressure not to keep them, not to feed them, and sometimes to outright kill them. People with disabilities brought stigma on the family.

I felt my jaw tighten with anger.

The poverty in the village and the conditions of their lives were very different from mine in the United States, but some things were so similar.

The fear.

The judgment.

Why, I thought, did people insist on seeing us as something less than human?

How could they possibly think that they had the right to decide who should live and who should die?

But no matter how much I hated it, I knew nothing would change until we changed it. Until we all stood up and demanded the right to live our lives like everyone else.

■ ■ ■

"How have things changed since you started organizing?" I asked the men and women in the village, the little child still playing with the marker at his mother's feet.

"Well, they're calling us by our names now," said a man, who was blind. "They used to just call us by our disability."

"Like Limper," said one.

"Or blind."

"Deaf," said another.

■ ■ ■

It was small, but it was a first step.

Like we'd been doing in America, the disabled people in India were learning how to use their voices and work with the leaders of the village to be heard. The disability rights movement was spreading. The same issues warrant the same tactics.

It was a beginning.

■   ■   ■

In another village in a different, remote part of India, I sat on the porch of a small house. Electric cords ran out the windows and stretched into the house next door, so the two homes could share electricity. The path in front of me led to a well, where a group of women and children gathered with buckets. The heat here felt different from the other village. It blasted, like I'd opened an oven door and stuck my head in to check on something.

A group of disabled activists surrounded me. Around them sat some women, the mothers of the children with disabilities, and they were fighting to get their children into school. Disabled kids weren't allowed into school in this village; they were denied the appropriate identification card that was required to register them. No identification card meant no education. No identification card meant they didn't exist.

The women reminded me of how many parents I'd met over the years, fighting for their kids' education.

They reminded me of my mother.

Again, their lives were so different from mine, but they cared about so many of the same things. They wanted their children to be treated with respect and dignity. They wanted their children to be treated fairly.

■ ■ ■

A later trip. This time to Uganda. And I found myself, again, in a village with dusty dirt roads, no running water and no electricity. In the center of the village, outside a small hut, I met with a group of disabled people. One person sat in a wheelchair. It was an old-fashioned wicker chair, like the one Franklin Roosevelt used in the 1930s and 1940s. Some other people sat with their young children, who appeared to have cerebral palsy. There was an older blind woman. As I always did, I started driving my motorized wheelchair around the circle to shake everyone's hand.

Suddenly, a wail filled the air.

"Why are you innnn really will you will him him him him him him him him him?"

My heart stopped. What was that?

We all looked around to see who was crying.

A boy, about two years old, clung tightly to his mother's leg, staring at me, his eyes enormous. He was frozen, petrified.

Hastily, I drove my wheelchair to take my place back in the circle. As my chair moved, though, he began wailing and crying again. Unsure of myself, I stopped moving. A flush rose in my face. I was embarrassed. The boy seemed to be afraid of me.

When I stopped moving, the boy stopped screaming.

When I moved forward, the boy screamed again.

Then my interpreter leaned over.

"I'm so sorry," he said, "he seems to be afraid of your chair."

And it hit me: the boy had never seen anyone in a motorized wheelchair before.

■ ■ ■

You should know that there is an international human rights movement, which I am a part of, that is making an effort to call attention to disability as a major issue.

But this didn't happen until 2008, when the United Nations created the Convention on the Rights of Persons with Disabilities. This international treaty agreement requires participating countries to promote, protect, and ensure the human rights of people with disabilities. Before 2008 there was almost no mention of disability anywhere as a global problem. There was almost no information being gathered on how many disabled people there were in the world and what they needed.

Nobody was paying attention.

Until we—all the disabled people from around the world—made them.

■ ■ ■

Even though change seems slow, like it's impossible and takes forever, and you are just one person up against an entire government, know this: activism makes a difference.

When we want to, we can turn the world on its head, provided we band together and we're willing to stay up until three in the morning and listen to every single person speak. Even if they speak one letter at a time with a pointer attached to their head.

■ ■ ■

Maybe you've seen stories about us on television or in the movies.

Maybe it's a movie about someone who becomes disabled and then wants to die.

Or maybe it's about someone else, who becomes disabled and turns villainous.

Almost always, the stories are a tragedy. Because someone else is telling them, not us. I don't think my life is a tragedy because I've had a disability.

■ ■ ■

Does having a disability make me different from how I would have been without a disability? I don't know the answer to that question. Or maybe I do and I don't, at the same time.

Would you be different if you'd been born Catholic or grown up in Sydney instead of San Francisco? How do you know?

What I do know is that I've had to learn to push through my insecurities.

I've learned I'm stronger in a group.

■ ■ ■

I know having my disability has given me opportunities I wouldn't have had otherwise. I wouldn't have been exposed to the same things.

I know it pushed me to study harder, work harder, and achieve harder. To travel.

I know it pushed me to fight. To change how others saw us. And what we could be.

Would I have met Ed and Frieda and Kitty and Eunice?

My life would have been totally different. And the same.

How does anyone know what their life would have been?

I can only know that it was meant to be what it was. I am who I was meant to be.

■ ■ ■

If I could, I would write a thousand stories about
disabled people, about everyone at the sit-in, every
protester, every activist in India, Uganda, and Sweden,
every one of my friends from Health Conservation 21.

Everyone who's ever been told that their story was
a tragedy.

Everyone who's ever been told that their story
didn't matter. Because the world wants to pretend they
don't exist.

How many movies or television series have you
watched with a disabled person in it?

How many movies or television series have you
watched with a disabled person in it, who wasn't
white? Or from the United States?

The world thinks that if you've heard one disabled
person's story, you've heard them all.

I hope my story about our protests is not the only
one you ever hear.

■ ■ ■

Actually, though, maybe I wouldn't write anyone's
story. Instead, I would ask those people if they might
tell their own stories.

Because how can we possibly know someone else's
story unless we listen?

ACKNOWLEDGMENTS

FROM JUDY AND KRISTEN

We would like, first and foremost, to thank all the amazing activists and supporters whose stories loom large in this book. Some of you are no longer with us, but we have felt your influence no less strongly.

We want to express enormous gratitude to the Rolling Warrior Youth Advisory Board (in alphabetical order): Will Dalzell, Jasmine Gallion, Becca Hadtrath, Anja Herrman, Abby Joiner, Oliver Ng, Isla Ramsden, Olivia Sandbrook, and Dominika Tamley. You met on weekend mornings, read multiple versions of this manuscript, provided invaluable feedback, gave fantastic writing suggestions, chose photos, voted on covers, and made us laugh! We cannot thank you enough.

We are indebted to HolLynn D'Lil Fuller and her self-published book *Becoming Real in 24 Days: One Participant's Story of the 1977 Section 504 Demonstrations for Disability Rights* and to the University of California at Berkeley Bancroft Library's Oral History Center project for their incredible foresight to interview the activists of the disability rights movement, both of which provided an invaluable record of events around the Section 504 sit-in.

This project would never have come to fruition without the spark provided by Jon Miller and Stuart James, who convinced Judy that she had a story that needed to be told and played matchmaker with us. Jill Marr, our agent at Sandra Dijkstra Literary Agency, and Kevin Cleary and John Beach of Gravity Squared Entertainment carried the project forward and cheered us on. Joanna Green, our editor, gave excellent editorial direction and feedback, and the entire team at Beacon has been wonderful.

FROM JUDY

I want to thank my husband, Jorge Pineda, for his ongoing support of me and my work. When I met him in 1991, in Eugene, Oregon, our worlds were forever changed. Our values are aligned in our love of family and our fight for equality. Jorge left his country to join me in mine, and this is something I will always appreciate. I have learned so much from him. He has given me a love of music and delicious food, and an understanding of the discrimination against Latinos, which continues despite their enormous contribution to the fabric of our country. We have traveled to Mexico, eaten many wonderful meals with his family, and spent time in amazing museums. I have been privileged with a close relationship with our nieces and nephews as they have grown up and visited us over the years. Recently we were talking about why we love each other, and he told me that I was a wonderful woman and an activist. This being said, I know that making enough time for each other is always a challenge. I'm sure he rues the day he ever got me my first smart device in the 1990s.

I would like to thank my friends who have supported me and encouraged me, over the past years, to tell my story. My story is similar to so many other peoples—those with and without disabilities. Telling our stories helps strengthen our ability to continue to fight against injustice. Sharing the stories about how we want our world to be—and then turning these dreams and visions into reality—is what we must all commit to doing.

I want to thank my mother and father, Ilse and Werner Heumann, for never giving up, and continuing to fight—both with me and for me. My mother, for her relentlessness and for being a role model who taught me in her own quiet and persistent way to fight for justice, not only in the area of disability but also against racial injustice. She taught me the importance of a diverse coalition. My father, for his belief in me and support of what my mother did, for all the meetings he drove us to and protests he and my mother attended, and for the number of times he drove me to my singing lessons with Dr. Dwyer.

My brothers, Joseph and Ricky, also helped me to become the person I am today.

FROM KRISTEN

I am tremendously grateful to my parents—Laurie Warnick Joiner and Brian Joiner—who taught me to tell stories, live by my values, and laugh as much as possible. I am grateful to my stepmother, Lynnie Clemens, for her lovely warmth and help. Pat and Cath Sandbrook, my in-laws, who always give loving support. My brothers, David and Kevin Joiner. To my sisters and my soul sisters Nancy Crull, Alyssa Maurer, Lucinda Treat, Jennifer McIver, Margot Szamier, Ilana Storace, Jennifer Ratner-Rosenhagen, Maura Minsky, Ernestine Heldring, and too many others to name here.

To my beautiful family, I thank you again and again. Julian, Oliver, and Olivia, you tolerated my disappearance for long hours, sat in my lap to help copyedit (Olivia), made smart storytelling suggestions (Oliver), engaged in lengthy discussions about discrimination (Julian), and, most of all, kept me from taking myself too seriously. And Jon Sandbrook, my husband, you gently snowplowed a path in our lives to make space for this—I'd be lost without you.

CREDITS

Page 4: Photo courtesy of Judith Heumann

Page 66: Photo by Evelyn Straus/*NY Daily News* via Getty Images

Page 77: Photo by Betty Medsger

Page 88: Photo by HolLynn D'Lil, author of *Becoming Real in 24 Days*

Page 119: Photo by HolLynn D'Lil, author of *Becoming Real in 24 Days*

Page 148: Photo by Betty Medsger

Page 171: AP Photo/Jeff Markowitz

ABOUT THE AUTHORS

JUDITH HEUMANN is an internationally recognized leader in the disability rights movement. Her work with a wide range of activist organizations (including the Berkeley Center for Independent Living and the American Association of People with Disabilities), NGOs, and governments since the 1970s has contributed greatly to the development of human rights legislation and policy benefiting disabled people. She has advocated for disability rights at home and abroad, serving in the Clinton and Obama administrations and as the World Bank's first adviser on disability and development. Connect with her on Twitter (@judithheumann) and Facebook (TheHeumannPerspective).

KRISTEN JOINER is a writer and activist who tries to tell stories that change how people see the world. Her writing on exclusion and belonging, inequality, and social change has been published in *Stanford Social Innovation Review*, *Stuff*, and other outlets. In addition to writing, she has cofounded an environmentally sustainable middle school and a youth media organization, producing films written by young people and winning the Henry Hampton Award for Excellence in Film & Digital Media and the Paul Robeson Award for Excellence in Independent Filmmaking. She lives in Auckland, New Zealand, with her husband and three children.